DRAMATIC MONOLOGUE

The dramatic monologue is traditionally associated with Victorian poets such as Robert Browning and Alfred Tennyson, and is generally considered to have disappeared with the onset of modernism in the twentieth century. Glennis Byron unravels its history and argues that, contrary to belief, the monologue remains popular to this day. Alongside the canonical figures of Tennyson and Browning, she includes in her analysis lesser-known poets such as Charles Kingsley and recently rediscovered women writers such as Augusta Levy and Charlotte Mew. By focusing on monologue's status as a form of social critique, the author successfully demonstrates the longevity and relevance of the form, and accounts for its current popularity due to the increasingly politicised nature of contemporary poetry with reference to the work of poets such as Ai and Carol Ann Duffy.

This refreshingly clear guide provides students with a compact introduction to a key topic in literary studies.

Glennis Byron is a Reader in English Studies at the University of Stirling. She is the author of *Letitia Landon: The Woman behind L.E.L.* (1995) and various articles on Victorian literature and the Gothic.

D1450308

THE NEW CRITICAL IDIOM

SERIES EDITOR: JOHN DRAKAKIS, UNIVERSITY OF STIRLING

The New Critical Idiom is an invaluable series of introductory guides to today's critical terminology. Each book:

- provides a handy, explanatory guide to the use (and abuse) of the term
- offers an original and distinctive overview by a leading literary and cultural critic
- relates the term to the larger field of cultural representation.

With a strong emphasis on clarity, lively debate and the widest possible breadth of examples, *The New Critical Idiom* is an indispensable approach to key topics in literary studies.

DRAMATIC MONOLOGUE

Glennis Byron

Routledge
Taylor & Francis Group

LONDON AND NEW YORK

First published 2003
by Routledge
11 New Fetter Lane, London EC4P 4EE

Simultaneously published in the USA and Canada
by Routledge
29 West 35th Street, New York, NY 10001

Routledge is an imprint of the Taylor & Francis Group

British Library Cataloguing in Publication Data
A catalogue record for this book is available from the British Library

Library of Congress Cataloging in Publication Data
Byron, Glennis, 1955–
    Dramatic monologue / Glennis Byron.
    — (The new critical idiom)
    Includes bibliographical references and index.
    1. English poetry—History and criticism. 2. Dramatic
    monologues—History and criticism. 3. American poetry—
    History and criticism. I. Title. II. Series.
       PR509.M6 B97 2003
       821'.02–dc21   2002155683

ISBN 978-0-415-22937-1

CONTENTS

SERIES EDITOR'S PREFACE

The New Critical Idiom is a series of introductory books which seeks to extend the lexicon of literary terms, in order to address the radical changes which have taken place in the study of literature since the last decades of the twentieth century. The aim is to provide clear, well-illustrated accounts of the full range of terminology currently in use, and to evolve histories of its changing usage.

The current state of the discipline of literary studies is one where there is considerable debate concerning basic questions of terminology. This involves, among other things, the boundaries which distinguish the literary from the non-literary; the position of literature within the larger sphere of culture; the relationship between literatures of different cultures; and questions concerning the relation of literary to other cultural forms within the context of interdisciplinary studies.

It is clear that the field of literary criticism and theory is a dynamic and heterogeneous one. The present need is for individual volumes on terms which combine clarity of exposition with an adventurousness of perspective and a breadth of application. Each volume will contain as part of its apparatus some indication of the direction in which the definition of particular terms is likely to move, as well as expanding the disciplinary boundaries within which some of these terms have been traditionally contained. This will involve some re-situation of terms within the larger field of cultural representation, and will introduce examples from the area of film and the modern media in addition to examples from a variety of literary texts.

ACKNOWLEDGEMENTS

This book would never have been completed without the help of an Arts and Humanities Research Board research leave grant, for which I am extremely grateful. I am also grateful to John Drakakis, the series editor, for his constructive comments and invariably helpful suggestions, and to Liz Thompson, Justin Dyer and Monica Kendall for all their help and patience. Thanks also to the other John for the occasional eighty-five amp blast which sent me out to the garden; to Tim, for the helpful if not always clearly recalled conversations (and the dramatic monologue is ....); and finally to Gordon, who provided the constant sunny intervals.

The authors and the publisher would like to thank the following for permission to reprint material:

Extract from 'The Love Song of J. Alfred Prufrock' in *Collected Poems 1909-1962* by T.S. Eliot. Reprinted by permission of Faber and Faber.

1

INTRODUCTION

A woman hangs upon a cross. Blinded, bleeding and wearing a crown of thorns, her husband hangs beside her. They are the Christian martyrs Saint Maura and Saint Timothy, and this is a poem by Charles Kingsley. Maura begins to speak to her husband: 'Thank God! Those gazers' eyes are gone at last!' (1); she speaks, straining credibility somewhat given her situation, for seven whole pages. He is silent, or rather silenced, since she anticipates and cuts off any possibility of interruption: 'No – you must not speak ... Now you must rest' (14, 16). Through Maura's words we are, nevertheless, made aware that the occasional groan and sigh escapes from her suffering husband as she recalls her part in the events that led to their crucifixion. When Maura remarks towards the end that in spite of her own suffering, 'my voice has never faltered yet' (222), for example, she then immediately pleads, 'Oh! do not groan, or I shall long and pray / That you might die; and you must not die yet' (223–4). He must endure the pain, she urges, and save his strength in order to be able to start preaching to the crowd which will gather the next morning; after all, 'they told us we might live three days ... / Two days for you to preach! Two days to speak / Words which may wake the dead!' (225–7). Poor Timothy, apparently less enthused by this prospect, decides it is time for a nap – 'Hush! is he sleeping?' (227) – bringing Maura's speech to its end. And just as well, the post-Monty Python reader might conclude, before a chorus pops up and breaks out in a rousing rendition of 'Always Look on the Bright Side of Life'.

Charles Kingsley's 'Saint Maura. A.D. 304' (1852) is not a particularly well-known poem; it certainly has not attracted the attention of any recent anthologists of Victorian poetry. Nevertheless, given this brief summary, those familiar with that central Victorian poetic form the dramatic monologue would be likely to agree in identifying the poem as an example of that genre. It is highly unlikely, however, that they would demonstrate similar accord when it came to defining what a dramatic monologue might be. As Herbert Tucker observes, dramatic monologue is one of those generic terms 'whose practical usefulness does not seem to have been impaired by the failure of literary historians and taxonomists to achieve consensus in its definition' (Tucker 1984: 121–2).

The term 'dramatic monologue' was not in widespread use until late in the nineteenth century, the poets initially demonstrating their own uncertainty about defining the new form in which they were working by naming their collections with such titles as *Dramatic Studies*, *Dramatic Lyrics* and *Dramatic Idylls*, and the critics adding to the confusion with such terms as 'mental' or 'psychological monologues'. Simultaneously drawing upon and reacting against the three primary poetic kinds, lyric, dramatic and narrative, the genre has resisted from the start all attempts at definitive classification, all attempts to impose uniformity, and what we now know as the dramatic monologue is a category that embraces a wide and diverse variety of forms. The problems of establishing any generic uniformity have recently begun to escalate as the general expansion of the Victorian poetic canon has started to have implications for the specific categorisation of the dramatic monologue. If the critics have failed to achieve any consensus in discussing the traditional canon of monologues, dominated by Robert Browning and Alfred Lord Tennyson, what happens when we begin to include such 'minor' writers as Kingsley or such women poets as Augusta Webster? This is a question to which I will be continually referring throughout this study.

 Ina Beth Sessions is usually considered to have initiated the drive towards fixing and codifying the dramatic monologue as a genre, and her taxonomic article of 1947 offers a useful starting point for clarifying the terms of the debate. Chapter 2 will consider some of the key moments in the history of attempts to define the dramatic monologue, and explore the ways in which the formal terms set out by Sessions have been interrogated and adapted as theoretical positions changed. Since Robert Browning is seen by Sessions and so many subsequent critics as the foremost practitioner of the dramatic monologue, and his 'My Last Duchess' (1842) as the paradigmatic form, I will trundle the duke back out on the stage once more and give him the attention and pre-eminence upon which he has insisted. In order to suggest how the interrogation of terms has begun to be intensified by the recent expansion of the canon of dramatic monologues, however, the duke will be placed in company he would be unlikely to find congenial, in particular with such speakers as the voluble Maura on her cross, Eulalie, the prostitute of Augusta Webster's 'A Castaway' (1870), and the maddened infanticidal mother of Elizabeth Barrett Browning's 'The Runaway Slave at Pilgrim's Point' (1848).

Chapter 3 will then move on to consider the origins of the dramatic monologue. While some critics have considered the form to belong to a poetic tradition that begins with the early Greeks, this is a position that has gradually lost favour. As genre theory has moved critical attention away from formalist concerns and towards questions of historical process, critics have begun to identify the dramatic monologue as the product of a particular set of cultural conditions. It is now generally believed to be a form that originates in the early nineteenth century, and which emerges primarily in reaction to Romantic lyricism and Romantic theories of poetry.

This is the first position that will be explored in Chapter 3, with particular reference to those poems of Alfred Tennyson and Robert Browning that are usually considered to be the first examples of the genre. As these seminal works show, the dramatic monologue begins as a poetry of contestation: by placing the speaking self in context, Tennyson and Browning expose the illusory nature of the autonomous and unified Romantic subject. The challenge to Romantic lyricism, however, also needs to be placed in a broader context of social and cultural change. Victorian literature generally moves away from an emphasis on the autonomous individual and begins to represent the self in context, focusing upon the individual in relation to others and upon the individual's position in society. Furthermore, the new mental sciences were further pushing the limits placed upon personal autonomy as they began to recognise that hidden dimensions of the mind could have significant consequences for the conscious self. The rise of the dramatic monologue was frequently considered by contemporary critics to be closely related to the emergence of these new schools of psychological thought. Turning to issues of gender, this chapter will conclude with an alternative look at possible origins by examining a recent challenge to the position that the form was first developed by Tennyson and Browning. The work of Felicia Hemans will be used as a test case for the claim of those critics who have begun to suggest that it might instead have been women poets writing during the transitional period of the 1820s who invented the monologue.

While this would appear to be a position that remains debatable, it is certainly true that gender issues play a significant role in the development of the dramatic monologue as a form, and Chapter 4 will address three main gender-related issues. The first section of this chapter will consider the way women poets use the monologue to critique conventional assumptions concerning the feminine and the innovative ways in which they manipulate the form. This will be followed by a section on men's monologues in order to demonstrate how, while gender remains a crucial issue, the main focus is not so much on masculinity as on the gendered dynamics of self and other. The cross-gendered monologue, which became a significant sub-genre and a particular interest of male poets, will then be examined, with particular reference to notions of role playing and performance. While there is no doubt that gender is an important issue in men's monologues, it is nevertheless true that it does not play quite such a dominant role as it does in women's monologues. The question that consequently needs to be addressed is whether men and women can be said to conceptualise and exploit the dramatic monologue differently. An emphasis on gender issues in women's monologues, I will argue, does not in fact place them within a different tradition; rather, it demonstrates that they are working primarily in that line of development which focuses on social critique.

Chapter 5 will move on to consider the two main lines of development during the nineteenth century, the historical and the social, and the innovative ways in which the form's central dynamic of self and context begins to be exploited. In the hands of such poets as Robert Browning and William Morris, that dynamic of self and context is brought together with the Victorians' concern to locate themselves within history, and narrative subsequently becomes an increasingly important element of the form. This historical line of development focuses primarily on questions of epistemology, that is, questions concerning the ways in which knowledge is produced and truth known. The dramatic monologue is exploited not simply to animate the past but also to interrogate history and the historical subject, to demonstrate that any attempt to reconstruct history will always be partial and interested. Questions of representation and interpretation consequently become central to the form, and the exploration of these questions leads to various developments in the genre. Browning, for example, experiments with multiple voices in *The Ring and the Book*, while such poets as Augusta Webster explore the possibilities of duologue, where two distinct but related monologues are juxtaposed.

Women poets like Webster, however, continue to be more particularly interested in the other line of development, in the social and polemical rather than the historical monologue. Their representations and interpretations of the self in context primarily serve the function of social critique. Opening up the canon consequently results in a need to rethink our overall assessments of the dramatic monologue as a form. The recovery of monologues by woman poets, and by 'minor' male poets, has demonstrated that polemic was far more important than traditional criticism has allowed. In light of this recognition, the work of such poets as Algernon Charles Swinburne, with his constant attack on the ideological constructs of his age, becomes as important to the evolution of the form as the work of Robert Browning. As the final chapters will begin to suggest, it is the social and polemical line of development that has survived most vigorously up until the present day.

At the end of the nineteenth century, as the Aesthetes and Decadents turned back to the lyric in their explorations of states of intense self-consciousness, interest in the dramatic monologue began to decline. Modernist poets such as Ezra Pound and T.S. Eliot initially appropriate the form for the purposes of experimenting with poetic voice, but out of these experiments a new kind of poem begins to evolve, and the speaking 'I' fragments into a multiplicity of voices. In the past, critics have generally considered this to mark the end of the dramatic mono-logue as a significant poetic form; after this, it is usually agreed, the monologue is put only to occasional use. As Chapter 6 will argue, how-ever, assessments of the decline of the monologue in the Modernist period are based primarily on the work of a small number of canonical and primarily male poets. Once again, opening up the canon to include 'minor' poets suggests a slightly different story. The elusive and imper-sonal voice cultivated by such poets as Pound and Eliot was of little use to those more overtly political poets, both men and women, for whom identity was still something that needed to be established. Although the dramatic monologue was by no means the central poetic form during the first part of the twentieth century, the work of such poets as Charlotte Mew and Langston Hughes suggests it survived in a far healthier state than is generally assumed, and that it did so primarily as an instrument of social critique.

Furthermore, as the final section of Chapter 6 will suggest, the 1960s saw a gradual revival of interest in the dramatic monologue. Richard Howard, for example, following in the tradition of Browning, began to use the form to engage with and interrogate history and the historical subject. Looking back to the historical past, however, Howard's monologues appear somewhat anachronistic in comparison with Edwin Morgan's work within the genre. In his direct exploration of contemporary events and concerns, his concern with the destabilisa-tion of the self and his engagement with the media, Morgan anticipates many of the ways in which the form will subsequently develop in the late twentieth century.

The last twenty or so years have seen a striking resurgence of interest in the dramatic monologue, and Chapter 7 will suggest that this is at least partly due to the increasingly politicised nature of contemporary poetry and its status as social discourse. As an increasingly accessible poetic form, the dramatic monologue is now considered particularly appropriate for the purposes of social critique. The historical line of development continues to have some influence, but primarily in those revisionist monologues that draw upon characters from literature, his-tory or myth. Such monologues, frequently marked by an overt femi-nist politics, focus on the ways in which cultural beliefs are fixed and formalised. Unlike earlier monologues, they present an incongruous 'I' which conflates the historical or fictional speaker's world with the contemporary world of the writing poet, consequently drawing more attention than ever before to questions of representation. Perhaps the most striking feature of contemporary monologues, however, is the way in which they have been influenced by the rise of a global electronic media. Contemporary monologues not only exploit various types of media discourse, they also frequently appropriate specific people, events and issues publicised by the media. The 'I' who speaks in today's monologue is quite likely to be the man or woman splashed across yesterday's headlines. The path that leads from Browning's 'Porphyria's Lover' (1836) to Ai's 'The Good Shepherd: Atlanta, 1981' (1986), Carol Ann Duffy's 'Psychopath' (1987) and Ken Smith's 'Brady at Saddleworth Moor' (1990), however, no longer seems quite as clear and direct as the critics who describe such poems as 'Browningesque' might believe. This study, then, will consider the development of the dramatic monologue from its nineteenth-century origins to the present day. Throughout, the focus will be upon the ways in which recent theoretical and canonical developments have challenged traditional understandings of the genre. In order to understand the nature of these challenges, however, it is first necessary to establish the main terms of the debate, and it is to this question that I will now turn in the following chapter on definitions.

2

DEFINITIONS

SETTING THE TERMS OF THE DEBATE

Ina Beth Sessions's taxonomic article on 'The Dramatic Monologue' (1947) is usually considered to have initiated the drive towards fixing and codifying the dramatic monologue as a genre, and offers a useful starting point for clarifying the terms of the debate. Responding to the marked differences in early critical opinion as to what constituted a dramatic monologue, Sessions focused on its formal features to offer a working definition of the 'Perfect' dramatic monologue which would include seven definite characteristics: 'speaker, audience, occasion, revelation of character, interplay between speaker and audience, dramatic action, and action which takes place in the present' (Sessions 1947: 508). As an example of such a 'Perfect' form, Sessions offered 'My Last Duchess'. So enters the duke, our speaker, and the envoy, our audience or auditor; and, without problematising the terms of Sessions's definition for the moment, consider how neatly the monologue slides into place. The 'occasion', the 'concatenation of circumstances which initiates the action of the piece' and 'provides the background and the personalities involved' (509), is that the duke is negotiating a marriage settlement with the envoy of the count, whose daughter he wants for his next wife. The dramatic action involves the duke showing the envoy a painting of his last wife, and this action unfolds in the present, so the reader feels like an observer of the original occasion, watching something in process:

> That's my last Duchess painted on the wall,
> Looking as if she were alive. I call
> That piece a wonder, now: Frà Pandolf's hands
> Worked busily a day, and there she stands.
> Will't please you sit and look at her?
>
> (1–5)

While only the duke speaks, interplay between speaker and auditor is clearly indicated: the duke's words frequently reveal that he is responding to comments made by the envoy. The envoy must, for example, have inquired about the expression on the duchess's face, since the duke refers to others for whom he has drawn the curtain which hangs in front of the portrait, 'Strangers like you' who have 'read' that 'pictured countenance' (6–7) and turned to him

> And seemed as they would ask me, if they durst,
> How such a glance came there; so, not the first
> Are you to turn and ask thus. Sir, 'twas not
> Her husband's presence only called that spot
> Of joy into the Duchess' cheek.
>
> (11–15)

Showing leads to telling, and the duke now begins to comment upon his wife's character. The glance, the spot of joy, he suggests, could easily have been caused by any flattering comment from the painter since his wife had

> A heart – how shall I say? – too soon made glad,
> Too easily impressed; she liked whate'er
> She looked on, and her looks went everywhere.
> Sir, 'twas all one!
>
> (22–5)

Everything would 'draw from her alike the approving speech, / Or blush at least', the duke continues, 'as if she ranked / My gift of a nine-hundred years-old name / With anybody's gift' (32–4). And then, the crucial revelation:

> Oh sir, she smiled, no doubt,
> Whene'er I passed her; but who passed without
> Much the same smile? This grew; I gave commands;
> Then all smiles stopped together. There she stands
> As if alive.
>
> (43–7)

According to Sessions, the duke reveals so much about himself to the envoy, including the fact he probably had his wife murdered, in order to ensure the information is passed on and the next duchess will give him the attention and respect he believes to be his due; if she does not, she is likely to end up in an adjoining frame. The dominant interest of the monologue, it soon becomes apparent, is the speaker's revelation of his own character, and whether he intends it or not, he emerges as egotistical, materialistic, controlling and cruel.

'My Last Duchess' can be said to 'splendidly illustrate all' (508) of Sessions's characteristics, she believes, but perhaps there is something of the chicken and egg about all this: it may illustrate, but it simultaneously circumscribes and delimits, the 'Perfect' form. Her prescriptive approach certainly sets out such a stringent set of conditions that many other poems generally discussed as dramatic monologues cannot be accommodated within the definition, and, in recognition of this, Sessions offers a set of 'sub-classifications', including the Imperfect, the Formal and the Approximate dramatic monologue, which demonstrate a progressive loss of one or more of these characteristics.

Given the drive towards fixing, codifying and establishing hierarchies apparent in Sessions's definition, it was perhaps inevitable that there should be almost immediate resistance and an eventual dismissal of this formulation as reductive and restrictive. While subsequent critics chafed against the prescriptiveness of her definition, however, perhaps the main problem was not necessarily a matter of limits and restrictions. This is certainly suggested when Sessions's definition of the dramatic monologue is placed alongside M.H. Abrams's description of what he

called the 'greater Romantic lyric', the other primary poetic expression
of the speaking 'I'. Such a lyric, Abrams writes, presents

> a determinate speaker in a particularized, and usually, a localized,
> outdoor setting, whom we overhear as he carries on, in a fluent ver-
> nacular which rises easily to a more formal speech, a sustained collo-
> quy, sometimes with himself or with the outer scene, but more
> frequently with a silent human auditor, present or absent.
>
> (Abrams 1965: 527–8)

As the similarities in the definitions of the two poetic types suggest,
more than a formal list of characteristics is likely to be required in the
definition of any genre. What is most strikingly obscured here is our
sense of the very different natures of the speakers in these two forms.

POET AND SPEAKER

Precisely because the two poetic types have such close formal connections, much of the subsequent debate centred on distinguishing the dramatic monologue from the lyric, in particular determining the different
natures of the respective speaking 'I's, and the relationship of those
speaking 'I's to the actual poets. While Abrams calls lyrics 'fragments of
reshaped autobiography' (Abrams 1973: 123), closely linking speaking
voice to poet, from the start the speaker of the dramatic monologue has
been distinguished from the figure of the poet. Reading Wordsworth's
'Daffodils' (1807), we may well assume it is the poet himself who wan-
dered 'lonely as a cloud' (1), but we are unlikely to connect Browning
with the duke or Kingsley with Saint Maura. A nod needs to be given
to the New Critics here, since the influence of the New Critical dogma
about the 'persona' still lingers and could problematise even this broad
point about the dramatic monologue. The New Critics claimed that all
poetry maintains certain dramatic features and that the poet always
speaks in an assumed character and an assumed situation; this position
would tend to eliminate all distinctions between the lyric and the
dramatic monologue. Most critics would now agree, however, that
while both lyric and dramatic monologue present a first-person speaker,

there are some significantly different *tendencies* in the two forms, and they have different effects, even if, in some texts, they begin to merge.

In his influential *The Poetry of Experience* (1957), Robert Langbaum moved away from the formalist emphasis on technical features to consider the two types of poems in terms of their power of affect. Langbaum's basic suggestion was that the dramatic monologue originates when Victorian poets write a Romantic lyric of experience in the voice of characters separate from their own. While we are invited to share the speaker's emotions in such lyrics as Wordsworth's 'Tintern Abbey' (1798), and encouraged to accept the poet as a guide to experience, we are supposed to stand back in order to analyse the speaker of a dramatic monologue in much the same way as the poet stands back rather than offering us direction. Ralph Rader makes a similar point when he distinguishes dramatic monologues, such as 'My Last Duchess', from dramatic lyrics, such as Keats's 'Ode to a Nightingale' (1820), by suggesting that, in the former,

> the reader must imagine the speaker as an outward presence, as we in our bodies register others in their bodies, from the outside in, whereas in the dramatic lyric we are imaginatively conflated with the speaker, understanding him from the inside out, seeing with his eyes and speaking with his voice as if on our own behalf.
>
> (Rader 1984: 104)

As Rader himself admits, however, different readers might not agree on which speakers do or do not have this cinematic effect. What is important about such attempts to describe variations in dramatic 'I' poems is the way they try to sharpen our sense of the nature of the 'I' who speaks. What is potentially problematic, given that readers and conventions of reading change, is the way so many of these attempts depend upon a fixed reader response.

In recognition of this, critical attention has attempted to focus closely on the signals found on the page. In the lyric, there are no signals to the reader that the speaker should be distinguished from the poet; on the contrary, there are more likely to be signals that encourage conflation of poet and speaker. Reading Wordsworth's 'Tintern Abbey', most readers are happy to label the speaker 'Wordsworth', while allowing that the poet has made certain choices about how to present himself as speaker, and few would not identify 'dear sister' as Dorothy Wordsworth, even to the extent of reacting critically, in both senses of the term, to the ways in which Wordsworth chooses to present her. With the dramatic monologue, however, there are, to varying degrees, always signals that we should not conflate poet with speaker.

In some poems, these signals are unmistakable. The distinct world of the speaker may be established through a wide variety of means, some, although not all, of which may be immediately indicated in the title; these include distancing the speaker temporally and culturally, as in Kingsley's 'Saint Maura A.D. 304' and Barrett Browning's 'The Runaway Slave at Pilgrim's Point', appropriating a known historical, literary or mythical figure, as in Tennyson's 'Ulysses' (1842) and Webster's 'Circe' (1870), and the provision of a language recognisably specific to a speaker, as in Browning's 'Fra Lippo Lippi' (1855) or one of Tennyson's 'Northern Farmer' monologues (1861, 1866). Sometimes it is a matter of cross-gendering: a woman writes as a man or a man as a woman: Algernon Swinburne becomes 'I, Sappho' in 'Anactoria' (1866), for example, and Browning writes as 'James Lee's Wife' (1864). In the latter poem the speaker is not only distinguished from Browning by gender but also conveys the illusion of being a very specific character. With 'A Woman's Last Word' (1855), however, the fact that we know it was written by Robert Browning plays a significant part in our definition of the poem as dramatic monologue since the speaker is only vaguely particularised. When Adelaide Anne Procter responds with her version of 'A Woman's Last Word' (1858), we are on less certain ground: since the speaker is again only vaguely particularised, there are no longer any signals to prevent poet merging into speaker and becoming the lyric 'I'.

In any case, not all speakers of dramatic monologues are quite as clearly particularised as in most of the previous examples, and when that is the case then the difference from the lyric speaker tends to be less easy to define. In this respect Alan Sinfield, drawing upon the idea of the 'feint' developed by Käte Hamburger in her exploration of fictional narrators, has been particularly helpful. Sinfield, whose 1977 monograph offered the first full-scale reassessment of the form since Robert Langbaum's *The Poetry of Experience* (1957), starts from the very broad position that dramatic monologues are 'first-person poems where the speaker is indicated not to be the poet' (Sinfield 1977: 42). Then, he sets up a distinction between a first-person lyric, where the reader is given 'the illusion at least of direct access to the experiencing poet' and the third-person narrative, which posits at least two levels of person: the one described and the one describing. The dramatic monologue, he suggests, 'lurks provocatively between these two forms' (24). 'Dramatic monologue feigns because it pretends to be something other than what it is: an invented speaker masquerades in the first person which customarily signifies the poet's voice' (25). There are signals that the speaker is not the poet, pushing towards fiction; the use of the first-person mode, however, pushes towards the lyric 'I' and suggests a real-life existence for that speaker. What is particularly useful about Sinfield's concept of the feint is that it allows for a number of complex variations on the dramatic monologue to be identified. A poem like Matthew Arnold's 'Dover Beach' (1867), where there are few signals that it is not the poet speaking, on this scale, moves the feint towards the poet's 'I'; indeed, many might argue against this being a dramatic monologue at all. Conversely, in a poem like 'My Last Duchess', establishing in detail a world that is clearly not the poet's, the feint begins to approximate to fiction and no one would mistake it for the lyric voice. The idea of the feint also allows Sinfield to make such poems as Tennyson's 'Oenone' (1832) or 'The Lotus Eaters' (1832), both of which are introduced by third-person narrative, less problematically dramatic monologues since the feint, he argues, can go on to reassert itself.

For Sinfield, the view of critics who suggest we are encouraged to believe in the actuality of the speaker is quite categorically wrong; apart from the fact that this is, he argues, 'an impossible reading experience' (30), in the 'dramatic monologue we feel continuously the pressure of the poet's controlling mind' (30). At the most basic level, this pressure is often felt through the poem's form, which repeatedly draws attention to its condition as text. The speech of Browning's duke, with its hesitations, interjections, questions, and disclaimers, may show various signs of oral discourse; the gruff speakers of Tennyson's 'Northern Farmer' poems may present themselves in an even more colloquial and naturalistic way through the rough dialect of Lincolnshire. Nevertheless, with both the duke and the farmers, we remain aware they are speaking in rhyming couplets, a clear signal of the artificiality of the speech act and the guiding hand of the poet. In fact, as a number of critics have observed, the more 'naturalistic' the monologue, the more obtrusive the shaping hand of the poet becomes, since the more our attention is drawn to those signs which do point to the poem's condition as text. We therefore understand 'the "I" of the poem as a character in his own right but at the same time sense the author's voice through him' (Sinfield 1977: 25). What we experience in the dramatic monologue is therefore a 'divided consciousness': we are always aware that the speaker is a dramatic creation and that there 'are other possible, even preferable, perspectives … we are obliged to posit simultaneously the speaking "I" and the poet's "I"' (32). And so Sinfield comes to a conclusion reached by many other critics of the dramatic monologue: that the one thing dramatic monologue is *not* is monological.

For some critics, a sense of division or splitting is specifically linked to the emergence of dramatic irony as a result of the disjunction between the limited understanding of the speaker and the wider awareness of the poet and the reader. The speaker's meaning can always be distinguished from the poem's meaning, or, as Robert Langbaum puts it, 'the meaning of the dramatic monologue is in disequilibrium with what the speaker reveals and understands. … we understand, if not more, at least something other than the speaker understands' (Langbaum 1957: 146). The implication here is that we can distinguish the voices of two distinct subjects for a single discourse: that of the poet and that of the speaker.

Kingsley's 'Saint Maura' lends itself to such a reading. Maura speaks at such length in order, she claims, to 'while away the hours till dawn' (22) for her husband. The main subjects upon which she focuses, however, the anxiety, humiliation and suffering she has endured, suggest more is at stake than diverting Timothy, and certainly the crucial placement of some of his sighs and groans suggests he is far from entertained. The groan that follows Maura's declaration that 'my voice has never faltered yet' (222), for example, may well be the result of the agony of crucifixion, but it may equally be the agony of being unable to escape that endless voice and the wish that, after seven pages of monologue, it *would* falter. What gradually emerges is Maura's driving need to reassert the authority of her own sense of self, to reassert her integrity, after a failure of faith. The desire to save both herself and her husband led to her agreeing to persuade her husband to renounce his faith and hand over the Sacred Books which the Roman authorities under Diocletian were attempting to seize and burn. Timothy's response, as she recalls it, 'Traitress! apostate! dead to God and me' (66), deprives her of both identity and voice: 'I could not speak – / I could not speak for shame and misery' (74–5). When she refused to help the authorities further, she was subjected to public humiliation, stripped and whipped before being sent to be crucified by her husband's side. Now, redefining her failure of faith as momentary madness, she speaks urgently, repeatedly, and at length of what she endured: she strives to establish herself as the 'lost lamb returned, / All re-baptized in blood' (26–7) in order to define herself in Timothy's terms as 'martyr' and re-establish herself as 'wife once more' (28). Read in this way, 'Saint Maura' could be said to open up the space for dramatic irony by suggesting that we, poet and reader, understand the speaker more clearly than she understands herself.

Monologues which exploit dramatic irony indicate the presence of a double-voiced discourse, two differently oriented speech acts within the same words. This has occasionally led critics to see the dramatic monologue as anticipating the principles of dialogism as argued by the Russian literary critic Mikhail Bakhtin. For Bakhtin, language is not singular and monolithic but plural and multiple, always containing many voices. However, the presence of dialogism or the play of different voices in a monologue is not necessarily dependent upon a split between poet and speaker. And as the canon of monologues has expanded over the past few decades, it has become clear that this particular kind of split is not always a characteristic of the form. Even with Browning, whose poems are often amenable to being read in terms of dramatic irony, Loy D. Martin argues that this is only one of various ways in which a sense of doubleness or discursive splitting may emerge (Martin 1985: 110–11). With a number of dramatic monologues, even though a clearly fictional character speaks, readers are left with the sense that the basic position proposed by that speaker is fully endorsed by the poet. Martin offers a useful point of clarification here. 'The division between the voice of the poet and the voice of the imaginary speaker', he writes, is based on a reader's willingness to construe them both equally as 'persons'. If these persons are imagined to be corporeal, then they must be discrete, mutually excluding entities. But if they are voices and merely voices, can they not in some sense be both different and the same?

(Martin 1985: 110)

This is certainly the case with such overtly political monologues as Barrett Browning's 'The Runaway Slave at Pilgrim's Point'. Written in response to a request from friends in the American anti-slavery movement, the monologue was first published in 1848 in the abolitionist yearbook *The Liberty Bell* and displayed at the Boston National Anti-Slavery Bazaar. The speaker has endured the murder of her lover, rape by her white master, and the subsequent birth of a 'too white' (116) child whom she has killed. As the poem opens she has travelled to the site of the pilgrim landing in Massachusetts, where 'exile turned to ancestor, / And God was thanked for liberty' (3–4), in order to curse the land that was once blessed in the name of freedom. Obviously, this speaker and the poet Barrett Browning are discrete entities, separate 'persons', but as 'voices' they share much, though not all, and could be said to begin to merge in the poem's critique of slavery. Dialogic relations are introduced here not through the presence of dramatic irony which distances poet from speaker but through the speaker's resistance and challenge to the systems and forms of discourse which justify and perpetuate racial oppression. When the slave asserts, with reference to the infanticide, 'I am not mad, I am black' (218), she, along with the poet, challenges the dominant definitions of both madness and blackness.

The silent but nevertheless clearly heard voices of repressive authority are rendered dialogical even more explicitly in another highly politicised monologue, Webster's 'A Castaway'. At one point the prostitute speaker Eulalie picks up a religious tract which offers itself as the monological voice of definitive truths and meaning, 'Where is it? where's my rich repertory / of insults biblical?', and then proceeds to ridicule the text for its clichéd and old-fashioned representations:

> *'I prey on souls'*
> Only my men have oftenest none I think:
> *'I snare the simple ones'* – but in these days
> There seem to be none simple and none snared.
> ...
> *'I braid my hair'* – but braids are out of date:
> *'I paint my cheeks'* – I always wear them pale:
> *'I –'*
> Pshaw! the trash is savourless to-day.
>
> (154–62)

While the tract attempts to define and fix both the moral and physical nature of the prostitute's 'I', Eulalie's interjections repeatedly relativise, parody and thereby dialogise the text of the 'windy dullard' (164) whose words she eventually consigns to the fire.

According to Isobel Armstrong, however, the tendency of dialogism to emphasise a rather straightforward opposition between voices limits its usefulness for discussions of the dramatic monologue. Armstrong offers a more subtle and convincing explanation of the sense of division produced by this form in *Victorian Poetry. Poetry, Poetics and Politics* (1993). She considers dramatic monologue to be the primary example of what she calls the 'double poem', a form which includes such other types of poem as the framed narrative or the dream. Utterance in the double poem, she writes, is seen both as subject and object, allowing 'the poet to explore expressive psychological forms simultaneously as psychological conditions *and* as constructs, the phenomenology of a culture … such a reading relates consciousness to the external forms of the culture in which it exists' (Armstrong 1993: 13). The struggle between the two kinds of reading is much more dynamic and complex than that suggested by Bakhtin's dialogic form; it is not simply 'a question of a simple dialogue or dialectic form in which the opposition between two terms is fixed or settled' (14). Rather, lyric description and analysis are repeatedly redefining the terms of a question and contending for its ground' (15). 'The gap between subjective and objective readings', she continues,

> often initiates a debate between a subject-centred or expressive and a phenomenological or analytical reading, but above all it draws atten-

tion to the act of representation, the act of relationship and the medi-
ations of language, different in a psychological and in a phenomenological world.

(13)

Armstrong's concept of the double poem can account for the sense of
division even in such monologues as 'The Runaway Slave at Pilgrim's
Point' or 'A Castaway', where, as voices, poet and speaker appear to
share much in their challenge to the official discourse. With both
monologues, the subject-centred or expressive reading draws attention
to the link: both Barrett Browning and Webster could be said to merge
with their speakers in their scathing judgements on society. At the same
time, however, the phenomenological reading goes far beyond the feelings and experience of the speaker upon which the expressive reading
focuses. A phenomenological reading draws attention to and analyses
the forms by which consciousness is made manifest or externalised
rather than its internal condition. It demonstrates how much the
speaker, unlike the poet, is caught up in and has internalised large por-
tions of those discourses that the expressive reading shows both she and
the poet are challenging. Barrett Browning's slave may reject the idea of
difference which is used to justify white superiority, but she nevertheless
has come to see herself in white terms as a commodity (Parry 1988:
124). Similarly, Eulalie may present an astute analysis of her society, but
she has accepted more of the social discourse of the prostitute as corrupt
than she is aware. 'For all her clarity of perception,' Angela Leighton
notes, 'the Castaway cannot see *herself*' (Leighton 1992: 200). What
both monologues consequently expose is relationships of power: language reveals the individual to be formed by the very society she critiques.

Although the speaker of a dramatic monologue is never the homoge-
neous poetic self of the pure lyric, therefore, the form is now considered
to allow for various positionings of the speaking subject with respect to
the writing poet. Consequently, while many recent critics find a certain
'doubleness' or 'discursive splitting' to be a recognisable feature of the
dramatic monologue, they suggest that the clear separation of poet from

speaker is only one of many ways in which doubleness may be produced in the dramatic monologue. As will already have started to become apparent in the preceding discussion, the emphasis changes from difference *between* to difference *within*.

READER AND AUDITOR

Most Victorian dramatic monologues feature an auditor who must, in order for the monologue not to slide into dialogue, remain silent, or at least unheard by the reader, since interventions and responses from the auditor are sometimes implied by the speaker's words. When Fra Lippo Lippi says, 'Who am I? / Why, one, sir, who is lodging with a friend' (14–15), he is clearly responding to (and repeating) a question that has been posed to him. Sometimes, non-verbal responses are suggested, as when Hiram Horsefall, the irate auditor of Browning's 'Mr Sludge: "The Medium"' (1864), responds with an action we know of only through Sludge's outraged 'Aie – aie – aie! / Please, sir! your thumbs are through my windpipe, sir! / Ch-ch!' (16–18). Critical opinion on the function of the auditor has been divided and the degree to which the auditor is essential to the form can be questioned. While Ina Beth Sessions claims that without an audience 'there would be no *genre* as has been defined in this paper' (Sessions 1947: 512–13), she does not really explain why. 'It is essential', she suggests, 'that interplay be active between the speaker and audience, constantly contributing to the flow of ideas' (509). But 'flow of ideas', as a monologue like Webster's 'A Castaway' clearly demonstrates, is not dependent upon the presence of another.

It is sometimes suggested that the presence of an auditor serves to challenge the apparently monological voice, to dialogise the speech and imply the possibility of other perspectives than the one we are offered by the speaker. The suggestion of other perspectives, however, does not actually require there to be a living auditor with the potential to respond. In 'My Last Duchess', it could be argued that the count's envoy who serves as the duke's audience would have a different perspective to offer, that he might not see the duke quite as the duke himself does, and the very fact he is there but remains silent could prompt speculation about his response. At the very least, the presence of this silent envoy might prompt us to consider why a duke, who supposedly chooses 'Never to stoop' (43), should be revealing so many intimate details to someone who is basically a servant, and this might encourage us to question the authority of the duke's perspective on events. But we would probably be prompted to do this anyway, and primarily by the presence of the dead duchess herself, captured and fixed in the portrait on the wall, but yet looking 'as if she were alive' (2), still animated by a half-flush, a significant glance. It is the duchess who most forcefully challenges the authority of the duke's speech with her strangely animate yet inanimate presence and her perspective that would be most threatening to the duke's vision of himself and his world. While auditors may imply the possibility of other positions, therefore, this is a more general function of the overall context, the context of which an auditor is only a part.

More frequently, considerations of the function of the auditor are linked to the role of the reader. The dramatic monologue, with its absence of any clear guiding authorial voice, seems particularly designed to provoke reader response, and almost from the start the reader has been considered to have a significant role to play. The reader is crucial to Robert Langbaum's definition of the dramatic monologue as a form which posits a <u>disequilibrium</u> between sympathy elicited for the speaker and moral judgement. For Langbaum, analysis of the speaker of a dramatic monologue focuses on analysis of the resulting tension experienced by the reader. As his definition relies so heavily on the work done by the reader, Langbaum's approach might be considered a precursor of reader response criticism. While highly influential for a number of years, Langbaum's ideas in this respect are now increasingly questioned, however, primarily because readers frequently find themselves hard-pressed to sympathise in any way with many speakers of dramatic monologues or indeed to pass moral judgement on many others. Langbaum's argument relies upon the kind of reader that has become increasingly difficult to accept in the wake of the destabilisation of the self that has marked poststructuralist, postcolonial and feminist theory.

As Cynthia Scheinberg has recently suggested in her analysis of the complexities of sympathy (Scheinberg 1997), the problem becomes particularly clear in Langbaum's reading of 'My Last Duchess'. 'What interests us more than the Duke's wickedness is his immense attractiveness',

Langbaum claims, and we 'suspend moral judgement because we prefer to participate in the Duke's power and freedom, in his hard core of character fiercely loyal to itself' (Langbaum 1957: 83). But who is this 'we'? To which 'us' does Langbaum refer? Many of 'us' may well be puzzled by his readerly capacity for sympathy with the duke. The difficulty lies in his assumption of some universalised reader, in his failure to acknowledge that sympathy and judgement will always be predicated as much, if not more, upon the reader's specific cultural, historical and social identity as on the language and strategies of the poem itself. Certainly few critics today are willing to agree with his sweeping assertion that 'we allow [the duke] to have his way with us' (85). In spite of this curiously sexualised image, Langbaum's universalised 'we' is implicitly male. A woman reader's questioning of patriarchy might preclude any possibility of sympathising with the 'power and freedom' which authorises turning a woman into a wall hanging. Subsequent critical response to the poem has demonstrated that many of 'us' – female *and* male – are not so easily seduced.

The roles of auditor and reader are brought together by such critics as Dorothy Mermin in her book *The Audience in the Poem*. Mermin, who limits her discussion of audience to the present and conscious kind, the kind we might expect to interrupt at any moment, argues that using an auditor becomes 'the poet's way of incorporating into the poem the reader he wants or fears, and trying out ways of talking to him' (Mermin 1983: 8). One significant difference between auditor and reader needs to be acknowledged. The auditor is in a state of enforced silence and, usually, passivity; the reader, however, is forced into active response. John Maynard, focusing on Browning's monologues, suggests that the silent auditor can be seen as a kind of 'poetic gadget' which provokes us to 'break into our own noisy response'; the very silence of Browning's envoy in 'My Last Duchess' becomes a hook to pull us into action, a way of provoking reader participation in the process (Maynard 1992: 74). Maynard is not interested in defining 'the ideal interpretive position'; instead he insists that we need to 'explore the range of response – experiences – the poem generates' (76); we need to 'read the reader' (77). The form not only contextualises its speaker, it also has the interesting ability to force us, as readers, to contextualise ourselves, to remind us that we too are the products of particular social and cultural conditions. The crucial question becomes not so much what we see when we read but why we see what we do.

The auditor, then, could be said to play a significant role in the way the dramatic monologue brings to the fore and dramatises the problematic issues of interpretation. 'My Last Duchess', where the duke places the envoy before the painting as interpreter as we are similarly positioned in front of the poem, provides an example of how questions of interpretation can be literally foregrounded. We could see him as an internal representative of the reader since we both, envoy and reader, watch the duke struggle – and not for the first time, we suspect – with the mystery of his last duchess, the 'meaning' of whom has so persistently eluded him.

The problem with the ideas about the function of the auditor considered so far is that in all cases the same end could be, and often is, achieved through other means. Many poems generally discussed as examples of the form either do not contain an auditor, as with Browning's 'Childe Roland to the Dark Tower Came' (1855) or Webster's 'A Castaway', or they make the use of the term 'auditor' problematic, as when Swinburne's poor scribe in 'The Leper' (1866) has only a wasted corpse by his side or Dante Gabriel Rossetti's young man addresses a sleeping prostitute in 'Jenny' (1870). Can the auditor then be oblivious or entirely omitted and the poem still function as a dramatic monologue, or do we need to find some other category, such as soliloquy, in which to place such poems?

According to Loy D. Martin, all monologists tend at least to project and fantasise a listener. These are still acts of communication and directed 'towards the problem of social interaction and its fragility' (Martin 1985: 138). These poems remain full of the markers of communication, those questions, demands and appeals which appear directed outwards; rather than suggesting simple internal debate, they emphatically remain representations of speech, even when interior monologue is implied, and in this way still announce themselves as dramatic monologues. To this can be added a more general point about the way genres develop. Once the form and a certain set of conventions have been established, then drawing on the conventions in order to announce the form and yet nevertheless transgressing against one of the established 'rules' is a way of drawing attention to an omission and may well serve a particular function. To insist upon placing dramatic monologues without auditors in a quite different category is to risk overlooking the way the text may be playing with the conventions of the genre.

Webster's 'A Castaway', for example, is very clearly signalled to be a speech act by markers of communication. In a literal sense, Eulalie nevertheless 'speaks' alone. This is not to say, however, that the convention of the auditor is simply ignored; Webster rather appears to be manipulating the reader's expectations. She draws the reader's attention directly to the omission with Eulalie's frequent expressions of desire for company: 'Will no one come?' (187) and 'So long alone! / Will no one come?' (453–4). Furthermore, we might want to ask why the monologue interestingly *ends* with the arrival of an auditor; the 'cackling goose' (626) who rings Eulalie's bell may not be the company she would prefer, but 'No matter; half a loaf /Is better than no bread' (628–9), and she greets her visitor with relief: 'Oh, is it you? / Most welcome dear: one gets so moped alone' (629–30). Both of these points direct attention to the fact that Eulalie has actually not been alone, but surrounded by the variety of past, present and future selves that her literal solitude prompts her to examine. Once a set of conventions have been established, transgression against these conventions tends to serve some function.

CHARACTER AND SUBJECT

Although Sessions is, generally speaking, rather vague about the function of the auditor, when it comes to the specific case of her paradigmatic monologue, 'My Last Duchess', the envoy plays a particularly important role. For Sessions, the 'best dramatic monologues' will 'reveal the speaker's character as the dominant interest' (Sessions 1947: 511), and the duke, she argues, reveals himself intentionally to the envoy in order to influence the behaviour of his next duchess, and by so doing, he also reveals himself to us. Whether the duke reveals this deliberately to the envoy is perhaps debatable. Is he, as critics have variously suggested, 'witless' in implying that he had his last wife murdered, or 'shrewd', ensuring his next wife will be made aware she must be a little more attentive and respectful? The idea that dramatic monologues primarily present unintentional and unconscious revelations has exerted the most influence on approaches to the genre, and still retains a surprising amount of power. One of the most recent studies, W. David Shaw's *Origins of the Monologue: The Hidden God*, offers a refinement on this account in arguing that the speakers are 'unconscious self-deceivers' (Shaw 1999: 167), that is, they deceive others because they do not themselves understand the truths about themselves or their situations.

The main problem with readings that emphasise revelation of character is the supposition that it is the reader's task to identify some essential character which might be revealed, either consciously or unconsciously, through the monologue. Such readings make a number of assumptions that many would now find questionable about the stability of the 'self' and the priority of this self to language. Language is seen to speak for some authentic character rather than the originating and authentic self being seen as an effect of language. The most significant change in approaches to the dramatic monologue during the 1980s and 1990s resulted from the postmodern attack on the idea of the autonomous subject and the accompanying growing interest in how the self is constituted. Readings of the dramatic monologue have been revolutionised by the understanding that, as Herbert Tucker observes, '[t]exts do not come from speakers, speakers come from texts' (Tucker 1985: 243). The supposed originating self of a dramatic monologue, after all, 'is the most elaborate illusion of the text, the product of a speech act and not its producer' (Tucker 1984: 134). 'At the same time, however,' Tucker adds, 'the ghost conjured by the textual machine remains the articulate phenomenon we call character: a literary effect we neglect at our peril' (Tucker 1985: 243). The illusion of a character does remain, but that illusion is a textual effect; we are offered a subject to be scrutinised but we simultaneously see this subject in process.

Ina Beth Session's initial proviso that the action should be dramatic, that it must be 'unfolding with the speaker's words' and 'in the present time', therefore remains important for contemporary critics. This is not so much for the sake of 'dramatic effectiveness' (Sessions 1947: 511), however, as for the way it allows us to observe the self as both process and product. The very fact that the dramatic monologue is by its nature a temporal fragment, focusing upon a particular occasion, emphasises that what we observe is only part of a larger process: something has gone before and something will follow. Frequently, this point is emphasised by the openings and endings of monologues, which either directly or indirectly indicate events already in progress, as in Browning's 'Bishop Blougram's Apology' (1855): 'No more wine? then we'll push back chairs and talk' (1), or events to come, as when Webster's Eulalie concludes by greeting a guest 'Oh, is it you? / Most welcome dear: one gets so moped alone' (629–30). The same effect may be created by references to what has been said or done outside the temporal moment of the text, as when Browning's duke says, 'I repeat' (48) and 'as I avowed / At starting' (52–3). All these strategic uses of language serve as a reminder that what we are offered is incomplete, only a small part of a larger process. The emphasis moves from what is 'expressed' to what is constructed, from what the text means to how the text works, from what is represented to ways of representation. It also leads to a consideration of the dramatic monologue in terms of performance.

As Dorothy Mermin observes, a 'dramatic monologue with or without an auditor is a performance: it requires an audience' (Mermin 1983: 11). In her view, however, the 'monologue lacks the resources to develop the temporal dimension, the notion of life as a continuing process of growth and change' (10). More recently, Cornelia Pearsall has brought together the ideas of process and performance in her reconsideration of the genre as a form distinguished by transformative effects. In opposition to the still dominant view that speakers of dramatic monologues reveal more than they intend, Pearsall argues that 'a major feature of this poetic genre is its assumption of rhetorical efficacy' (Pearsall 2000: 68). Speakers have particular purposes, specific goals, which they not only describe but 'also labor steadily to achieve through the medium of their monologues'; in reading such poems, therefore, 'we must ask what each poem seeks to perform, what processes it seeks to set in motion' (68). For Pearsall this is specifically related to the speaker's desire for transformation – 'of his or her circumstances, of his or her auditor, of his or her self, and possibly all these together' (71). In Browning's 'The Bishop Orders His Tomb at Saint Praxed's Church' (1845), for example, the bishop orders his tomb in the sense of instructing the sons he addresses, and in the sense of imaginatively designing the tomb through his monologue. The tomb, as the bishop himself suspects, may never actually be built, but this, Pearsall argues, is to some extent irrelevant. As the bishop stretches out his feet 'straight as stone can point' and lets the bedclothes 'drop / Into great laps and folds of sculptor's-work' (88, 90), the tomb begins to emerge before our very eyes.

CHANGES IN THE CANON

Pearsall's rethinking of the dramatic monologue as a genre which 'seeks to dramatize, as well as to cause, performative effects' (79) does not account only for the processes at work in the traditional canon of monologues. It also helps explain why the form became so frequently appropriated for polemic in those cases, such as Barrett Browning's 'The Runaway Slave' and Webster's 'A Castaway', where speaker and poet begin to merge in their attempt to 'create reactions and larger social transformations in the world outside the poem' (79). A notable feature of Pearsall's essay is that she brings women writers like Webster and Barrett Browning together with such canonical figures as Tennyson and Browning, not to suggest any gendered distinctions, but to discuss all these writers as practitioners of the monologue.

The work of women poets has rarely been included in the general theoretical discourse on the dramatic monologue, and while it is hardly surprising to find that women writers are not considered by such early critics as Sessions and Langbaum, it *is* surprising to see how frequently they remain ignored by those more recent critics who have benefited from the historical recovery and scholarly reconstruction of women's poetry which has taken place over the past few decades. The only woman mentioned in *Victorian Poetry*'s 1984 special issue on the 'dramatic "I"' poem was Elizabeth Barrett Browning, and that was not as a writer of monologues. More recently, in her 1996 monograph on the dramatic monologue, Elizabeth Howe mentions only one pre-twentieth-century woman poet, Christina Rossetti, who barely manages a page of her own, while W. David Shaw's *The Hidden God* (1999) similarly focuses on the traditional canon, bringing in Barrett Browning, but completely ignoring the key woman writer of dramatic monologues, Augusta Webster.

Articles discussing the monologues of such poets as Webster, Amy Levy, Elizabeth Barrett Browning and Charlotte Mew are, however, beginning to appear, and their work will be considered, along with the work of male poets, throughout the following chapters. Incorporating the works of women poets into more general discussions of the form may well result in our accepted ideas about the dramatic monologue being qualified or challenged. Generic grouping is a matter of historical process, not of fixed categories, and any system of classification serves the particular purposes of a group of critics or readers. The traditional canon of dramatic monologues was formed in retrospect by twentieth-century critics, based upon a selective group of texts, and colluded in the establishment of Browning and Tennyson as the canonical Victorian poets. Once the experiments with personae found in the works of such early nineteenth-century women poets as Felicia Hemans and Letitia Landon are recovered, along with the later dramatic monologues of such poets as Webster and Levy, the grouping becomes subject to redefinition, and new relationships among the texts are found, serving, necessarily, the purposes of a new group of critics and readers.

If the most significant recent change in approaches to the dramatic monologue has resulted from the postmodern attack on the idea of the autonomous subject and the accompanying growing interest in how the self is constituted, the most significant future changes may result from the adjustment of the generic grouping to include women's poetry. This process of recovery is still in its early stages, however, and in bringing together the works of male and female writers in my discussion of the dramatic monologue, I remain aware of the fate of the articulate fossil in May Kendall's 'Lay of the Trilobite' (*VWP*) (1887). Comparing the state of his species to that of mankind, the trilobite recalls how

> gentle, stupid, free from woe
> I lived among my nation,
> I didn't care – I didn't know
> That I was a Crustacean.
>
> (49–52)

But as Kendall soberly observes in a footnote, 'He was not a Crustacean. He has since discovered that he was an Arachnid, or something similar. But he says it does not matter. He says they told him wrong once, and they may again.' In the case of the dramatic monologue, the evidence is by no means all in. Some of my crustaceans may well turn out to be arachnids.

3

ORIGINS

THE INFLUENCE OF GENRE THEORY

While all would agree that the dramatic monologue came into its own during the Victorian period, there have been two main schools of thought concerning its origins: one focuses on the Victorian age itself, the other looks to a poetic tradition extending back to the early Greeks. Alan Sinfield, for example, takes the latter, inclusive position. He links Victorian dramatic monologues with such complaints as Theocritus's complaint of Polyphemus (third century BC) and Shakespeare's 'A Lover's Complaint' (1609) and with dramatic epistles from Ovid's *Heroides* (*c.* first century BC) to Pope's 'Eloisa to Abelard' (1717), saying of the poems he lists, 'I see no essential difference of form and prefer to consider all first-person poems where the speaker is indicated not to be the poet as dramatic monologue' (Sinfield 1977: 42).

Sinfield's all-inclusive position was characteristic of most influential approaches to the dramatic monologue during the 1970s and 1980s, and the predominance of this position seems to have been closely connected with more general approaches to genre. As David Duff notes, the modern period has been characterised 'by a steady erosion of the perception of genre, and by the emergence of aesthetic programmes which have sought to dispense altogether with the doctrine of literary kinds or genres' (Duff 2000: 1). Perhaps the most notorious attack on genre comes in French philosopher Jacques Derrida's influential essay on 'The Law of Genre', where he reacts against precisely the kind of approach to genre typified by Ina Beth Sessions's classification of the dramatic monologue. This essay, first translated in 1980, draws attention to what Derrida called the 'authoritarian summons to a law of "do" or "do not"', which, he claimed, 'as everyone knows, occupies the concept or constitutes the value of *genre*' (Derrida 1992: 224). Genre, he suggests, is inevitably involved with limits: 'as soon as genre announces itself, one must respect a norm, one must not cross a line of demarcation, one must not risk impurity, anomaly or monstrosity' (224–5). By the early 1980s, genre theory appeared to have been completely discredited. Critics of the dramatic monologue around this time tended to avoid the problems of generic criticism either by focusing on the works of one particular poet so as to avoid making general claims about form or, like Sinfield, by assuming the all-inclusive approach which places the dramatic monologue in a long-standing tradition. Little has been done to explore this tradition since it was first fully set out by Benjamin Fuson in *Browning and his English Predecessors in the Dramatic Monolog* (1948), and those critics who take this position tend to focus upon establishing formal similarities rather than tracing contextual development. An adequate account of the precursors of the Victorian dramatic monologue would need to consider the various historical moments in which these first-person poems arise, something far beyond the scope of this monograph.

While agreeing with Sinfield that all the poems he lists are part of the same tradition, I would not subscribe to his preference for considering as dramatic monologues all first-person poems where the speaker is indicated not to be the poet. As Langbaum argued earlier, 'While such a classification is *true* enough, what does it accomplish except to identify a certain mechanical resemblance? – since the poems retain more affinity to the lyric, the drama, the narrative than to each other' (Langbaum 1957: 76). To see generic categories purely in terms of formal characteristics is to dehistoricise a piece of work, and to treat it as an autonomous aesthetic object rather than something which is produced within specific material circumstances. As we will see, it is precisely this kind of isolation from context against which the earliest dramatic monologues reacted in the construction of the speaking 'I'.

Despite the discrediting of genre during the 1970s, there was a continuing attempt to recuperate the concept by those who argued for genre as a far more dynamic phenomenon than Derrida would allow. While Derrida finds an authoritarian imperative within the word 'genre' that requires to be resisted or deconstructed, in 'The Origin of Genres', first published in 1976, Tzvetan Todorov asserts that resistance comes from within the works themselves, that genres develop only through crossing lines, risking impurity; the

> fact that a work 'disobeys' its genre does not mean that the genre does not exist ... in order to exist as such, the transgression requires a law – precisely the one that is to be violated ... the norm becomes visible – comes into existence – owing only to its transgressions.
>
> (Todorov 1990: 14)

A 'new genre', he argues, 'is always the transformation of an earlier one, or of several: by inversion, by displacement, by combination' (15).

When genre is seen as something dynamic and historically determined, a fluctuating phenomenon, simultaneously marked by stability and fluidity, similarity and difference, attention is directed away from rules and conventions to historical process. This involves a consideration of why particular forms emerge, decline or change in particular cultures at particular times, and an emphasis on how genres develop within the cultural contexts of their production. Most critics now, while recognising that the dramatic monologue evolves out of other forms, would nevertheless argue for difference, difference expressed not in formal terms but through taking into account both the function and the ideological dimensions of genre. An interest in the political and cultural conditions of its emergence and development has inevitably led to a movement away from the all-inclusive position and towards seeing the dramatic monologue as a literary form that, as E. Warwick Slinn observes, 'was utterly immersed in the cultural conditions of its time' (Slinn 1999: 313).

REACTING TO THE ROMANTICS

The dramatic monologue is usually considered to be developed simultaneously but independently by Alfred Tennyson (1809–92) and

Robert Browning (1812–89) in the 1830s. Alternately, Tennyson invented it first, reading 'Saint Simeon Stylites' to a group of friends in 1833 (published 1842), but Browning was the first to publish, with 'Porphyria's Lover' and 'Johannes Agricola in Meditation' appearing in the *Monthly Repository* in 1836. Corroborating Todorov's position that a new genre is always a transformation of earlier genres, the dramatic monologue emerged primarily in reaction, and as an alternative, to other kinds of writing. Romantic lyricism, with its emphasis on the individual subjectivity of the poet, was the main poetic inheritance of the Victorians. As E. Warwick Slinn notes, while critics now tend to focus on the 'disruptive counterside of Romantic writing' and to demonstrate 'the struggles of the speaking subject to establish authenticity' in the Romantic lyric, the dominant literary inheritance of the Victorian poets was nevertheless 'a lyric voice which presented itself as autonomous, self-conscious, atemporal, and male, and an aesthetic which promoted the possibilities of transcendence, of attaining through metaphor a universality not bound by time, class, or gender' (Slinn 1999: 309). The dramatic monologue is generally accepted as the primary form through which Victorian poets began to negotiate both voice and aesthetic; the precise ways in which it does this, however, much like the nature of the form itself, have been much debated.

The condition of the age

Robert Langbaum and J. Hillis Miller offered the two earliest influential attempts to explain the emergence of dramatic monologue in terms of the age itself. Their focus was upon the differing reactions of the Romantics and the Victorians to the growing decline of belief in absolute values during the late eighteenth and nineteenth centuries. Established knowledge was increasingly challenged by developments and discoveries in science, most notably, perhaps, by emerging theories of evolution, which undermined religious faith and replaced the relatively comforting notion of change as cyclic repetition with the disconcerting idea of radical and unpredictable transformation. A world of uncertainties led both to a loss of coherent faith and to a loss of any stable position from which to speak.

According to Robert Langbaum, while the Romantics responded by turning to subjective experience in a search for transcendent truths and stable values by which to live, the Victorians, sceptical about such transcendent truths, developed the dramatic monologue to explore a variety of positions; it became an appropriate form 'for an empiricist and relativist age, an age which has come to consider value an evolving thing dependent upon the changing individual and social requirements of the historical process' (Langbaum 1957: 107–8). There are truths and judgements offered, but these are placed within their historical context and therefore shown to be relative, the product of a particular age. J. Hillis Miller also refers the emergence of the dramatic monologue to the loss of absolute values. According to Miller, however, trying out a range of beliefs, reliving 'one by one, all the possible attitudes of the human spirit', was for the early Victorians a means towards attaining a more 'absolute vision' (Miller 1963: 107) rather than a way of establishing all judgements as tentative. While Langbaum places the Victorians in opposition to the Romantics, then, Miller ultimately relocates the Victorians within the Romantic aesthetic of poetic transcendence and organic unity. For Miller, the Victorians, much like the Romantics, considered poetry to offer a means of transcending a world characterised by flux and disjunction and attaining a position of stability and authority from which some absolute truths could be discerned.

More recent critics have usually agreed in seeing the uncertainty of the age as being partly responsible for the emergence of the dramatic monologue, even if they have disagreed about what this condition produced. E. Warwick Slinn, for example, argues that in conjunction with this condition of uncertainty, 'poetic forms shift in emphasis. Rather than discovering completed wholes, we find structures that stress movement toward an end but where the attainment of that end is shrouded in incertitude' (Slinn 1999: 48). From this position, with its emphasis on process and incompletion, the dramatic monologue should not be positioned as backward-looking in terms of a return to a Romantic aesthetic of unity and wholeness, but as reacting against such an aesthetic and instead anticipating, and moving towards, a postmodernist culture of endless differentiation. Speakers in dramatic monologues may express the desire to discover truth, achieve goals, but like the title subject of

Tennyson's 'Ulysses', they repeatedly discover that the 'margin fades /
For ever and for ever when I move' (20–1).

The subjective–objective dichotomy

Underlying the theories of both Langbaum and Miller is the idea that
the form develops in reaction to the emphasis on subjectivity associated
with the Romantics. Many critics have seen the emergence of the dramatic monologue in terms of a movement away from the Romantic
emphasis on the subjective, on the poet's own experience and emotions,
and towards the exploration of a more objectively perceived world, of
what is external to the poet's mind. In *The Mirror and the Lamp* (1958),
M.H. Abrams influentially argued that the Romantics understood the
mind not as a mirror reflecting the external world but as a lamp project-
ing its light and creating as it perceives. This is something that the early
Victorians reacted against since, according to some critics, the

> fear implicit in Romanticism that we may fail to know the objects of
> our consciousness, that we may realize only an eccentric and per-
> sonal reality, motivates Victorian attempts to turn from what they per-
> ceive as a disabling focus upon the self.
>
> (Christ 1984: 5)

The authority for the position which explains the emergence of the dramatic monologue in terms of the subjective–objective dichotomy is often
found in the comments of the poets themselves. Browning, for example,
repeatedly claimed that his poems were, as he said in the 1852 advertise-
ment to *Dramatic Lyrics*, 'dramatic in principle, and so many utterances
of so many imaginary persons, not mine'. In his 1852 'Essay on Shelley',
he comments directly on the difference between the objective and subjective poet. The former, like Browning, represents things external as they
would appear to the common eye; he produces poetry which is 'projected
from himself and distinct': he is, in Browning's term, a 'fashioner' (King
1981: 5. 137). The latter, like Shelley, produces poetry which is 'the very
radiance and aroma of his personality, projected from it but not sepa-
rated': he is the 'seer', searching not for what man sees, but what God

sees. Concerned with 'the primal elements of humanity', he 'digs where he stands', seeking these elements within 'his own soul as the nearest reflex of that absolute Mind' (5. 138–9).

Although the subjective–objective distinction continues to be useful, the strictly oppositional stance it suggests has recently been qualified. It could be argued, for example, that many writers of monologues, particularly when the form is appropriated for social criticism, are conveying a particular and personal vision; in this sense their poems could be said to remain subjective. Furthermore, given Browning's own definition, the reader may well be tempted to define him as a subjective poet; in spite of the wide variety of speaking voices he employs in his monologues, as many have noted, it is generally quite easy to spot a Browning monologue and distinguish it from one, say, by Tennyson. Given an unidentified selection of their monologues, even first-time readers would be able to sort most of them out by author. Perhaps this is just a matter of style, but given the abstract and elusive nature of this term, it is difficult to separate the idea of style from 'the very radiance and aroma' of personality.

Most importantly, however, Alan Sinfield believes, the subjective–objective dichotomy can in itself be misleading: he refers to it as 'a product of Romanticism and one which it is by no means easy to clarify' (Sinfield 1977: 55). Sinfield's idea of the feint, discussed in the previous chapter, clearly shows that the dramatic monologue calls into question such easy distinctions, hovering as it does 'between the poet's "I" figure and an independent fictional world' (55). Authority for the problematising of the subjective–objective opposition can equally be found in the words of the poets themselves: Browning's comment about 'so many imaginary persons', for example, appears qualified by his address to Elizabeth Barrett Browning in 'One Word More', the dedicatory poem of *Men and Women* (1855):

> Love, you saw me gather men and women,
> Live or dead or fashioned by my fancy,
> Enter each and all, and use their service,
> Speak from every mouth, – the speech, a poem.
>
> (129–32)

The lines appear to suggest that the poet can simultaneously produce the utterances of 'so many imaginary persons' and yet still speak himself through their mouths. Elizabeth Barrett Browning's 'Runaway Slave' again offers a demonstration of the problem. The view of the inhumanity of slavery is very much that of Barrett Browning; is this, then, a 'subjective' poem because it conveys the poet's own vision? Or is it an 'objective' poem, either because it dramatises the experiences and feelings of a fictional character or because it constructs a more general and abstract criticism of slavery out of one particular woman's subjective responses to her experiences? Isobel Armstrong's theory about the Victorian double poem, discussed in the previous chapter, would suggest it is both. It is a subjective poem because it gives expression to the experiences of one particular individual slave, but simultaneously an objective poem because this subjective expression is offered as an object of analysis. Whatever position is taken, it seems clear that the subjective–objective dichotomy is at least problematised by the very nature of the dramatic monologue.

CONTEMPORARY THEORIES OF POETRY

Perhaps the most convincing explanation of the emergence of the dramatic monologue in terms of the age itself has been advanced by Herbert Tucker and further developed by Isobel Armstrong. Drawing specifically on the poems generally accepted as the first examples of the form to establish the starting points for their arguments, these critics suggest that the emergence of the dramatic monologue in the early Victorian age can be seen in terms of a cultural critique of contemporary theories about poetry, and this leads to an emphasis being placed upon the difference between Romantic and Victorian representations of the self. Philosopher and social critic John Stuart Mill reveals much about the prevailing views of poetry and the continuing dominance of lyric with his well-known pronouncement in an essay of 1833: 'Eloquence is *heard*, poetry is *overheard*.' 'Eloquence', he explains, 'supposes an audience; the peculiarity of poetry appears to us to lie in the poet's utter unconsciousness of a listener. Poetry is feeling confessing itself to itself, in moments of solitude' (Mill 1976: 12). The poet, he believes, can exclude from his work every trace of 'lookings-forth into the outward and every-day world'; if he turns around and 'addresses himself to another person; when the act of utterance is not itself the end, but a means to an end', then it is no longer poetry, but eloquence. The true poet, then, is sincere, unaware of an audience, detached from his context, while the orator is aware of, and interacts with, the world around him. Not surprisingly, for Mill lyric was 'more eminently and peculiarly poetry than any other' (36). To poets like Tennyson and Browning, Herbert Tucker suggests, this kind of poetry would have no doubt seemed overheard in a way quite different from that which Mill intended: 'heard overmuch, overdone, and thus in need of being done over in fresh forms' (Tucker 1985: 227).

The first dramatic monologues

Tennyson's 'Saint Simeon Stylites', written in 1833 and published in 1842, and Browning's paired poems of 1836, 'Johannes Agricola in Meditation' and 'Porphyria's Lover', to which he appended the title 'Madhouse Cells' in 1842, are usually considered the first published examples of the dramatic monologue and can all be seen, in varying ways, to offer a critique of Mill's position and its implications with respect to the representation of the self. While the lyric 'I' is supposed to inspire the reader's confidence in the voice that speaks, in all these poems the authority, integrity and autonomy of that isolated lyric voice are put into question. The speakers, Tucker argues with reference to Browning, are 'egotistical monomaniacs' who represent 'in overblown caricature precisely the unconstrained lyrical "I" whose private (and therefore sincere) utterances Browning's readership were sympathizing with' (Tucker 1984: 124–5).

In 'Porphyria's Lover', the speaker tells of the visit of the woman with whom he is clearly having an illicit relationship. As the pathetic fallacy of the opening immediately suggests, the external world exists for this speaker only as a projection of himself, and the reliability of what he sees is immediately questioned:

> The rain set early in to-night,
> The sullen wind was soon awake,

> It tore the elm-tops down for spite,
> And did its worst to vex the lake.
>
> (1–4)

In a world constructed in the speaker's own self-image, there is no room for reciprocity, for dialogue. When Porphyria arrives, makes the fire, takes off her wet clothes and finally sits 'down by my side / And called me' he remains silent: 'no voice replied' (14–15). Porphyria therefore attempts to take some control, arranges his arm around her waist, places his cheek on her bare shoulder, and spreads her yellow hair over him, 'Murmuring how she loved me' (21). The lover's reading of all this is, to say the least, excessive:

> Be sure I looked up at her eyes
> Happy and proud; at last I knew
> Porphyria worshipped me; surprise
> Made my heart swell, and still it grew
> While I debated what to do.
> That moment she was mine, mine ...
>
> (31–6)

A swift strangulation ensures she remains 'mine, mine', and suppresses any possibility of debate; the 'smiling rosy little head' (52), he can confidently declare, is 'So glad it has its utmost will, / That all it scorned at once is fled, / And I, its love, am gained instead!'(53–5). The attempt to establish authoritative subjectivity here necessitates the silencing of the other. Converted into an 'it', Porphyria's head can now be made to echo only the thoughts of her lover: 'its utmost will' is his. By so blatantly appropriating the consciousness of another in order to control meaning, the speaker loses any confidence we may have left in his authority and turns himself into the object of interpretation.

In this seminal dramatic monologue, there is no real auditor in the sense often expected of the form, no other voice with the potential to respond and challenge the position of the speaker. For Armstrong, this is part of the way Browning, both here and in 'Johannes Agricola', produces utterance as both subject and object:

> Characters so patently talking to themselves force a conscious inter-
> vention, force the reader to be aware of his or her exclusion and simul-
> taneously force that awareness into a consciousness of reading,
> understanding the poem as the object of analysis and thus as ideology.
>
> (Armstrong 1993: 145)

What, then, of the apparently anticipated response suggested by the
puzzling short phrase with which the speaker ends? Sitting with the
strangled Porphyria by him in a reversal of the positions she set up, her
head now on his shoulder, he returns to the present moment: 'And
thus we sit together now, / And all night long we have not stirred, /
And yet God has not said a word!' (58–60). God would seem to be an
irrelevancy in this world, constructed purely from the speaker's fantasies. Nevertheless, he does seem to be awaiting some kind of
response, and this peculiar final phrase again distances us from the
speaker, producing him as an object of analysis rather than authoritative voice. Why should he even mention God? Is it the possibility of
some divine reprimand, which might suggest at least some part of him
is aware that strangling one's girlfriend is not quite the thing to do.
The troublings of conscience implicit in this last line might then suggest the eruption of doubts, a suppressed voice within the self, the
emergence of a modern fragmented subject. On the other hand, it is
just as likely to be a divine note of congratulation he expects. He may
be mad, but he is not, as the phrase goes, out of his mind; he is too
entirely locked within it. If God were to speak, he could only, parrot-
fashion, speak the words of Porphyria's lover. Either way, the reader is
unable to retain any confidence in the authority and integrity of this
speaking 'I'.

That final phrase also takes us back to the communal norms, the
context, which the lyric is supposed to exclude. Mill's formulation of
poetry as entirely private experience imposes a barrier between poetry
and the external world which produces what Isobel Armstrong calls a
'poetics of exclusion' (Armstrong 1993: 137). The individual subject
communicates 'if at all by accidental empathy' (137). In the solipsistic
worlds of the first monological speakers, the external world would seem
to disappear, absorbed by the bloated self that speaks, and yet the claims
of the context Mill's formulation of poetry seeks to repudiate insistently

eassert themselves. We have quite a good idea what God might say to Porphyria's lover, just as we are sure that Porphyria would be unlikely to agree that this final interesting scenario is not precisely, as he would have it, the realisation of her 'darling one wish' (57).

The claims of context assert themselves even more persistently with the title speaker of Browning's 'Johannes Agricola in Meditation'. Agricola was the sixteenth-century founder of Antinomianism, which rejects the need to adhere to any moral law and predicates the salvation of the elect on faith alone. He believes himself one of the elect, and, since he has 'God's warrant' (33), feels himself so completely separate from and unaffected by the world that even if he were to drink a venomous cocktail blended from all 'hideous sins' (34), he knows his nature will convert / The draught to blossoming gladness first' (36–7). He believes, therefore, there is no need for him to act at all; time and place are irrelevant to him: 'I lie where I have always lain, / God smiles as he has always smiled' (11–12). But as Armstrong observes, such transcendence of the material world as Agricola claims is only possible because that material world exists (141); we are therefore repeatedly taken back to what he seeks to exclude. Similarly, Tennyson's Saint Simeon, based on a ascetic of fifth-century Syria, only appears increasingly enmired in the world he seeks to transcend in his quest for sainthood. Year in, year out, patiently poised on his lonely pillar, he lives through 'Rain, wind, frost, heat, hail, damp, and sleet, and snow' (16). As he repeatedly returns to the topic, climatic references peppering every subject he considers, this Syrian fanatic reveals an obsession with the weather to rival that of any Englishman. In his quest to achieve sainthood, he may attempt to reject the world, but the language of his monologue demonstrates how dependent he is upon this world in expressing any sense of self.

The Romantic idea that poetry expresses something sincere, some emotional truth, posits the kind of control over language that these early monologues repeatedly subvert. The poetic 'I' is shown to be, in Joseph Bristow's words, not 'a subject guiding language at will but a speaker who was, instead, *subjected* to language. The monologue indicates how *language* speaks over against the speaker' (Bristow 1987: 5). This is particularly clearly demonstrated by the ironic effect of Agricola's reiteration of the phrase 'I lie' in 'I lie where I have always

lain' (11) and 'For as I lie, smiled on, full-fed' (41). In various ways
therefore, these seminal works show how the dramatic monologue can
be said to begin as a poem of contestation, a ruthless taking apart and
exposure of the illusion of both the supposedly <u>autonomous</u>, authorita
tive and unified Romantic subject and the possibility of transcendence
of attaining a universal position untouched by context.

SELF IN THE BROADER CONTEXT

The challenge to Romantic lyricism needs to be placed within the con
text of broader material conflicts and changes. To begin with, the dra
matic monologue both influences and responds to a larger shift in
cultural models of the self. While scholars of Romanticism rightly
demonstrate that there were various competing models of the self dur
ing the period and that the self was always problematic, the dominant
inheritance bequeathed to the early Victorians was a model based on
the characterisation of the self in terms of psychological depth. This
concept of the self has its origins in the way the 'I' was defined by the
seventeenth-century French philosopher René Descartes. The Cartesian
cogito, 'I think therefore I am', leads to a separation of mind and world
with the inner self as the free autonomous centre of experience
Consciousness, in this understanding of the self, assumes a powerful
and controlling role, sifting through the images of the external world
that it receives, mediating, judging and producing meaning. It is also
during the early nineteenth century, however, that the idea of this
unconstituted subject, the separate and unified self of post-Cartesian
humanism, begins to be challenged. In *The Phenomenology of Mind*
(1807), the German philosopher Georg Hegel steered the investigation
of the self in a new direction when he proposed a theory of relational
identity: nothing exists in itself; identity is formed from or determined
by its relation with other identities.

Victorian literature generally reveals a movement away from the
autonomy of the individual in favour of representing the self in a rela
tional context. Such social critics as Thomas Carlyle repeatedly urge the
need to turn to the wider social world and place individual conscious
ness within the context of culture and the progress of history. The
1830s saw the development of such fictional forms as the 'silver fork

novel, the 'Newgate' novel, the social-realist novel, all notable for their strong emphasis on social markers, for their representations of the individual within a specific and highly particularised environment. The dramatic monologue, emerging during the same decade, can be said to follow the Carlylean imperative no less carefully than these diverse fictional forms, constructing a self that is not autonomous, unified or stable, but rather the unfixed, fragmented product of various social and historical forces.

In their concern to examine the self, the early Victorians inherited the tradition of introspection and self-analysis established by such thinkers as John Locke (1632–1704) and David Hume (1711–76); they also, however, challenged it. Introspection could well be fruitless, since, as the psychologist Alfred Maury observed in the 1860s,

> When once the mind of man is turned inwards, to the infinite, which he can neither grasp nor comprehend, he no longer perceives anything except his own sensations; he gazes as if in a magnifying mirror, which returns to him his own image.
>
> (in Faas 1988: 60)

The point had already been well demonstrated by such monologues as Browning's 'Porphyria's Lover', a poem which also demonstrates the even greater fear about introspection. 'Gazing inward on one's own self', as Thomas Carlyle observed, can indeed 'drive one mad' (in Faas 1988: 61).

The study of the self was becoming a new branch of scientific analysis in the early nineteenth century; it was not self-analysis, however, but the analysis of others that was the basis of the new school of mental science. Mental science, Ekbert Faas notes in *Retreat Into the Mind. Victorian Poetry and the Rise of Psychiatry* (1988), took in three disciplines: psychology proper, which studied normal consciousness in a state of basic sanity and grew out of the tradition of introspective analysis; mental pathology, which focused on abnormal states of mind; and mesmerism, which studied states of abnormal consciousness, such as somnambulism and clairvoyance, within the sane mind. The emergence of the dramatic monologue, Faas argues, is closely related to the rise of this new school.

Those poems usually considered the first dramatic monologues certainly show the importance of what Faas calls 'abnormal mental states', and it is no doubt significant that Browning's first monologues were placed under the heading of 'Madhouse Cells'. Deviance and abnormality would become a significant part of the tradition as the form developed; the poets moved into the darker areas of the mind, hovering, in the words of Browning's Bishop Blougram, 'on the dangerous edge of things' (395). Even those speakers who are in themselves not disturbed are frequently placed in extreme situations as though to examine the effects of such situations upon normal consciousness. As contemporary critical response to the poems demonstrates, the Victorians themselves considered the form to be essentially psychological poetry. They spoke, Faas notes, of ' "dramas of mental conflict," "dramas of the interior," of "mental monologues," "psychological monologues," "portraits in mental photography" and poems of a new "dramatic-psychological kind" ' (Faas 1988: 20). Contemporary critics such as H.B. Forman directly linked the emergence of this new psychological school of poetry to the rise of a new mental science, and the poems themselves were frequently discussed and reviewed in scientific journals. Tennyson, whose declared aim in *Maud* (1855) was to dramatise 'the history of a morbid, poetic soul, under the blighting influence of a recklessly speculative age', was particularly delighted when the poem was described in the *Asylum Journal of Mental Science* (1855–6) as ' "true example" of the "theory of the psychopathic origin of insanity" as recently outlined by the Belgian psychiatrist J. Guislain' (in Faas 1988: 13).

Of particular importance for the rise of the dramatic monologue was the growing recognition by mental scientists that hidden dimensions of the mind could have significant consequences for the conscious self. Studies of somnambulism and dreams began to explore states of mind in which there was a suspension of volitional control over thought processes. Rather than seeing consciousness as the basis of all mental activity, such psychologists as William Hamilton (1788–1856) were beginning to study the workings of the unconscious. Hamilton, for example, was the first to explore the process which would be later developed and popularised as 'unconscious celebration'. He noted the way in which one thought might rise immediately after another in consciousness without there being any apparent associative link between them;

this he explained by proposing an unconscious mental modification, a missing link B between the two conscious thoughts A and C.

Explorations of the limits upon personal autonomy by the mental scientists, along with the movement towards representing the individual in a relational context, point to changing conceptions of the self during the nineteenth century and can be said to initiate the movement towards our modern concept of the subject. As opposed to the notion of the individual self with agency and control over itself, the term 'subject' suggests an 'I' that is simultaneously a subject to itself within its own experience and always *subjected to* forces both outside itself, such as social and environmental forces, and within itself, the workings of the unconscious.

The emergence of the dramatic monologue as a form, therefore, needs to be seen as both a response to and an intervention in the specifics of a particular historical moment, especially in relation to the various changes in ways of conceiving and representing the self. Rather than rejecting the Romantic fixation on the self in quite the way that a straightforward understanding of the subjective–objective dichotomy might suggest, it is precisely the self with which the dramatic monologue remains concerned. 'What am I?' (124) asks Tennyson's Saint Simeon Stylites; 'Who am I?' (14) repeats Browning's Fra Lippo to the guard just prior to offering a long explanation; 'but what am I' (137) echoes the ageing woman of Webster's 'Faded' (1893); 'me. And what is that?' (26) adds her 'Castaway' to the chorus. Such questions recur with a striking insistence in dramatic monologues; over and over again they return to the conflicted issue of, in the words of the eponymous narrator of Tennyson's 'Tithonus' (1842), 'Ay me, ay, me' (50). The poets soon begin to exploit the form's central dynamic of self and context in various diverse ways, however, offering different models of, and evolving different strategic approaches to, the self. They dramatise it precisely in order to examine it, and in place of the autonomous self they propose and explore a more complex, fragmented and contextualised representation of the subject.

AN ALTERNATIVE THEORY

For an age which played such a central role in defining gender and sexuality as we know them, however, an age which conceived not only public and private but also economic and cultural production as gendered spheres, the 'self' could hardly be an unproblematic term. With this in mind, my last section on the origins of the dramatic monologue will consider the recent challenge to the generally held position that the form was developed by Browning and Tennyson in the 1830s by critics who have instead suggested that it might be women poets like Letitia Landon and Felicia Hemans, writing during that transitional period of the 1820s, who 'invented' the dramatic monologue (Armstrong 1993; Flint 1996). If this is true, then what might they have been reacting to and what specific functions might the monologue have served? In exploring these questions, I will focus on the work of Felicia Hemans, who, while now marginal to the canon, was in her own time much more central. Matched only by Scott and Byron in terms of popularity, she was able, after her marriage failed, to earn enough through her writing to support her five sons and her mother and eventually became the most published poet of the nineteenth century. Unlike Landon, whose reputation declined soon after her death, Hemans had a great influence on the Victorians, who would have been very familiar with her monologues, most of which are to be found in her collections *Records of Woman* (1828) and *Songs of the Affections* (1830). Hemans continued to be read until well into the 1890s, after which she became outdated and unfashionable; her monologues were forgotten and, until recently, she was remembered only for such anthology favourites as the much parodied 'Casabianca' (1829) ('The boy stood on the burning deck …') and 'The Homes of England' (1828).

The dramatic monologue would seem to be a useful form for a woman poet to develop given the attitudes towards poetry in general and women poets in particular which dominated the early part of the century and tended to linger throughout. To begin with, there was the traditional gendering of the speaking poetic subject as male and the object as female: the monologue offered one means by which women could assume the position of the authoritative speaking subject. More importantly, however, reinforcing the growing separation of spheres which linked women with the private and men with the public, there was the tendency to associate women writers with the personal and confessional, to see their writing as self-representational and concerned with the private world of the emotions. The assumption of a mask or persona might then be a strategy for self-protection: speaking in the voice of a dramatised 'I' is a way of insisting that the voice is not to be identified with her own, that her work *is* art, not simply an outpouring of personal feeling. In creating speakers for her monologues, Hemans achieves such distance by crossing boundaries of time and space, race and class. Her speakers include such specific historical characters as Arabella Stuart, imprisoned by James I after a secret, politically unacceptable marriage, and Prosperzia Rossi, an Italian sculptor. She also offers more general, anonymous types, in such poems as 'The Chamois Hunter's Love' (1830) and 'The Vaudois Wife' (1830). There are, therefore, many signals to the reader that the speakers are not to be identified with the poet Mrs Hemans, respectable Englishwoman.

Romantic women's voices

But if the use of the dramatised speaker is simply a distancing strategy, then, as Isobel Armstrong pointedly notes, why is there such an emphasis on 'speaking in another *woman's* voice' (Armstrong 1993: 325). Some qualification is necessary here, since many later women poets, including Augusta Webster, use male speakers as often as female. Nevertheless it is certainly true of such earlier women poets as Hemans and Landon. At the very least, Armstrong suggests, the use of the mask allows the woman writer to be 'in control of her objectification and at the same time anticipates the strategy of objectifying women by being beforehand with it and circumventing masculine representations' (326). What is puzzling, however, is if the use of the dramatic monologue offers women poets the possibility of circumventing men's representations of women, why then does Hemans appear to reproduce and confirm, rather than challenge, these representations? This is a question which could equally be put to Letitia Landon. In her emphasis on romantic rather than familial love, Landon might produce a female subject quite different from that of Hemans, but it is still a female subject who defines herself solely in relation to a man and a subject which reproduces male representations.

For Hemans's women, love and family are all. They are repeatedly presented as heroic, exalted over the male characters by their higher position on the moral scale and their superior capacity for love and self-sacrifice. The speaker of 'The Chamois Hunter's Love' (*VWP*), for example, recognises that the man she addresses may love her, but 'better, better far' (5) he loves his life in the wild snowcapped mountains and would not be happy living in the sunny green valley which is her home: 'thy path', she knows, 'is not as mine' (14). She, however, will give up her life for him, leaving family, friends and home. And her reward? Unfortunately not to gambol about the mountains with him; in Hemans's poetry, no matter what the culture or time depicted, the world is rigidly divided by familiar gendered roles. Instead, she will 'sit forsaken' (20) in his hut, listening in vain for his step at night, waking 'in doubt and loneliness' (33), praying for his safety. As the speaker herself is well aware, it is hardly an attractive proposition, but with a woman's love, stronger, truer, she is willing to sacrifice all for him: 'I would not change that lot; oh no! I love too well!' (25).

While Hemans may present women assuming the position of the authoritative speaking subject through her monologues, for the modern reader at least, it can be disturbing to recognise how completely they have internalised ideas which nevertheless efface any sense of themselves as individual subjects; the speaker of 'The Chamois Hunter's Love' is no more than what the title states, her self defined only through her relationship with her lover. Similarly, the speaker of 'A Spirit's Return' (1830) is so absorbed into the identity of the man she loves that 'There was no music but his voice to hear, / No joy but such as with *his* step drew near; / Light was but where he look'd – life where he moved' (73–5). As this suggests, there is one other way in which the woman's self is sacrificed in Hemans's work: her celebration of the woman as subject is achieved through the obliteration of the woman as subject. As the women are reduced to strangely depersonalised heroic types of wife or lover, mother or daughter, they become not so much individuals as abstract categories: they are women who demonstrate their natures through their capacity to love.

In this respect, while Hemans may distance herself from the speakers through time and place, she nevertheless identifies herself with these speakers by working from within the very constructions of female subjectivity she seems to be investigating. In constructing her own persona as 'poetess' she chooses, as Anne Mellor convincingly shows, to 'inhabit rather than reject the hegemonic construction of the ideal woman' (Mellor 1993: 107). Complicit in this hegemonic construction, that is, in one of her culture's dominant accounts of female subjectivity, she draws upon both lyric and narrative voice to write herself as the icon of female domesticity, celebrating home and hearth, the fidelity of women, the glory of maternal love. At the same time, she reproduces numerous variations on this self in the female speakers of those poems which could be considered early examples of the dramatic monologue. There seems, then, to be a challenge to the identification of women with the personal because the poet distances herself from the speaker by constructing a clearly fictional persona. Simultaneously, however, there is a confirmation of such an identification because the poet and the persona become conflated through their acceptance of a similar ideology and, specifically, through their commitment to an identical female subjectivity. As persons, the poets and their speakers may be quite distinct, but as voices, they are both different and the same.

'Prosperzia Rossi' (*VWP*), from the 1828 *Records of Woman*, is now Hemans's best known and most frequently reproduced monologue and offers a good example of these tactics at work. This is one of what have been called Hemans's 'self-mirroring' poems, engaging with one of her favourite topics, that of women and fame, and echoing many of the sentiments she herself expressed concerning her own position as a woman poet. The monologue is prefaced by a note of explanation which begins, at least, by making a gesture towards individualising the speaker: 'Prosperzia Rossi, a celebrated female sculptor of Bologna, possessed also of talents for poetry and music, died in consequence of an unrequited attachment.' Rossi is immediately distinguished by her profession, her nationality and her creative abilities. However, this information is grammatically placed in order to give the impression that it is an aside; the main clause of the sentence gives priority to the strength and endurance and all-consuming nature of her love, thereby linking her, in Hemans's world, to a wider community of women. The headnote is then followed by an unidentified quotation that also has the effect of downplaying the individuality of the woman. It begins with an immediate dismissal of talent – '*Tell me no more, no more / Of my soul's lofty gifts!*' – and the emphasis turns again to love:

> *Are they not vain*
> *To quench its haunting thirst for happiness?*
> *Have I not loved, and striven, and fail'd to bind*
> *One true heart unto me, whereon my own*
> *Might find a resting-place, a home for all*
> *Its burden of affections?*

The woman's failure to secure love serves to obliterate her identity: '*I depart, / Unknown*', she claims, '*though Fame goes with me*'. Achievement in the public world cannot validate her self as subject: she can only be 'known' if she is loved.

The voice of the opening explanatory paragraph which precedes these lines can be identified as that of Hemans, and the voice of the monologue which follows is clearly that of Rossi herself. But there is no indication of whose voice speaks in this epigraph, and so questions of identity are immediately complicated. It could be read as one of Rossi's own poems, because it anticipates the sentiments she goes on to express in such lines as

> ... give the reed
> From storms a shelter – give the drooping vine
> Something round which its tendrils may entwine –
> Give the parch'd flower a rain-drop, and the meed
> Of love's kind words to woman! Worthless Fame!
>
> (80–4)

To anyone familiar with Hemans's work, however, the voice could equally be identified as that of the poet herself; the sentiments certainly match those expressed in such lyric poems as 'Woman and Fame' (*VWP*) (1839):

> Thou hast a charmed cup, O Fame!
> A draught that mantles high,
> And seems to lift this earthly frame
> Above mortality.
> Away! to me – a woman – bring
> Sweet waters from affection's spring.
>
> (1–6)

Such linguistic connections are prevalent in Hemans's work, repeatedly being used to establish similarity in difference, to link women of all times, all cultures, in a vision of universal womanhood. She had already used these previously quoted lines from 'Woman and Fame' as an epigraph for her poem on 'Joan of Arc, in Rheims' (1828), who notably turns from the admiring crowd to the arms of her family, in much the same way as she uses the epigraph of 'Woman and Fame' in the last stanza of 'Corinne at the Capitol' (1830). The latter similarly strikes the familiar Hemans keynote: fame without love provides no satisfaction.

In Rossi's own monologue, further attempts are made to establish connections between women. Her last work is a depiction of Ariadne, the woman loved and then abandoned by Theseus. While the fates of Ariadne and Rossi are actually quite different, Rossi imposes similarity in difference: 'I give my own life's history to thy brow, / Forsaken Ariadne!' (37–8) she declaims: 'Thou art the mould, / Wherein I pour the fervent thoughts, th'untold, / The self-consuming!' (44–6). This depiction of her woe in the beautiful Ariadne, she hopes, may make the man she loved 'perchance regret' not returning her love, even, perhaps, prompt 'Sad thoughts' of her (126). As Hemans produces mirror images of her own persona in her dramatised female speakers, so Rossi produces a mirror image of herself through her art; Ariadne becomes to Rossi what Rossi is to Hemans. As all testify to the primary importance of love, love becomes 'self-consuming' in more ways than one. Forms of differentiation are overridden as individual identity is translated into type. And Rossi slips between the roles of subject and object: the woman as subject, as creative artist, uses that art to turn herself back to the more passive traditional female role she desires, which is that of an object: to desire is of little value; to be desired is all. Ultimately, Prosperzia Rossi is memorialised and celebrated by Hemans not because she was a 'celebrated sculptor of Bologna', a successful professional, but because she offers a representative example of woman's nature as essentially domestic, loving, self-sacrificing.

A conservative reading of Hemans's work, then, would suggest that her dramatised speakers serve not so much to question but to confirm conventional beliefs concerning female subjectivity. Speakers from a wide range of different times and places all testify to the importance of the domestic sphere and the affections, all define themselves primarily in relation to those they love. Hemans may cross the boundaries of time, culture, race and class in presenting her speakers, but she nevertheless repeatedly emphasises the almost indistinguishable essential nature of the individual subjects as *women*. Furthermore, these dramatised speakers echo the sentiments of the poet herself as voiced in both her lyrics and her interpretive commentary on other women's actions in her narrative poems. These monologues, therefore, serve a key role in the establishment of similarity in difference: they suggest that it is not just Mrs Hemans who defines or interprets woman in this way; her opinions are validated by the distinct historicised voices of other women apparently detached from the 'poet'. And by echoing Hemans, these speakers, by extension, speak directly to the validity of the sentiments and ideology of early nineteenth-century England. They consolidate the authority of the dominant cultural model of femininity.

As Cornelia Pearsall has noted, from the moment of their inception, 'dramatic monologues roam through much of the world and myriad historical periods', and in this way they can be seen as 'at once responding to and propelling the larger Victorian appetite for exploration and appropriation of other cultures' (Pearsall 2000: 73). If Hemans's poems are seen as early dramatic monologues, or at least precursors, then they would confirm Pearsall's point to an extreme degree. In terms of 'appropriation', Felicia Hemans has no match. Women's voices of all times and places are appropriated only to dissolve difference, eradicate individuality and create the illusion of an essential gendered identity, and, complicit with her culture, identify the essentially feminine as domestic, disinterested and self-sacrificing. It is surely no coincidence that she chose to name her best known collection of poems not *Records of Women* but *Records of Woman*. While context may become crucial to the construction of identity as the dramatic monologue develops, at this stage it appears significant primarily as a means of reinforcing the idea that in all times and all places, the nature of woman is fixed.

Of course, Hemans's ability to devote herself to the cultural work of defining the feminine as essentially domestic was only possible because she herself, with no husband and therefore no wifely obligations, living with a mother who took over most responsibilities for running the home and seeing to Hemans's five sons, encountered few of the problems with which this ideal feminine would inevitably find herself

plagued. William Wordsworth was apparently shocked and disapprov-
ing when Hemans visited and showed herself unable to use a needle and
completely uninterested in the matter of kitchen scales. But Hemans
was a professional poet, and she had a great deal of business acumen
and an eye for the literary marketplace. As the myth of saintly domesticity gradually grew around her, to be consolidated after her death in
memoirs written by her sister and the critic Henry Chorley, Hemans
contributed much to its development. In this respect there may be some
interesting connections between such early women poets as Hemans
and the emerging professional women analysed by Joan Riviere in her
influential essay of 1929, 'Womanliness as a Masquerade'. While seem-
ing 'to fulfil every criterion of complete feminine development' (Riviere
1986: 36), these women simultaneously 'fulfil the duties of their profession at least as well as the average man'. Women who 'wish for masculinity', Riviere argues, 'may put on a mask of womanliness to avert
anxiety and the retribution feared from men' (35). A similar 'anxiety'
might be detected in the works of such successful professional poets as
Hemans, and their self-images, their 'womanliness', may be seen as, in
Riviere's term, a 'masquerade'.

But there are cracks in the mask. While her female speakers yearn for
love, for the home and family, at the same time they frequently reveal a
stereotypical awareness of the satisfactions that result from self-fulfil-
ment, rather than self-sacrifice. This leads to the sense of division or
splitting in the subject that is characteristic of the dramatic monologue.
Prosperzia Rossi's obsession with a love that consumes her along with
her dismissal of fame and talent is qualified by the delight she expresses
in her creative powers, and the almost orgasmic descriptions of the creative process when the 'rushing train / Of glorious images' start to
'throng' and 'press' (29–30) upon her. The poem offers not so much a
straightforward dismissal of artistic talent as an awareness and exploration of the tensions and contradictions between the satisfactions
afforded by artistic creation and the satisfactions supposed to be
afforded by more normative feminine roles of wife and mother. It is
possible, then, that Hemans's dramatised speakers may serve a less conventional purpose than the previous reading would suggest.

In Hemans's poems we can see elements of resistance that critics
have begun to notice. Anne Mellor, for example, considers that while at

one level they may contain a celebration of a particular notion of female subjectivity, at the same time they provide a critique of its assumptions:

> having accepted her culture's hegemonic inscription of the woman within the domestic sphere, Hemans's poetry subtly and painfully explored the ways in which that construction of gender finally collapses upon itself, bringing nothing but suffering, and the void o nothingness, to both women and men.
>
> (Mellor 1993: 142)

Critics such as Anne Mellor and Susan Wolfson have shown that it is precisely those things through which the women define themselves, the home, the family and love itself, which are most threatened and unstable in this world. The home is usually something desired rather than possessed, and along with the celebration of the domestic ideal, there i an accompanying suspicion that it may be no more than a fiction.

To what extent, then, might Hemans's dramatised speakers function not only to confirm but also to resist or critique conventional ideology. The adoption of the mask in women's poetry, Isobel Armstrong argues involves 'a displacement of feminine subjectivity, almost a travestying o femininity, in order that it can be made an object of investigation (Armstrong 1993: 326), and it is this that creates the double form:

> The doubleness of women's poetry comes from its ostensible adoption of an affective mode, often simple, often pious, often conventional. But those conventions are subjected to investigation questioned, or used for unexpected purposes. The simpler the surface of the poem, the more likely it is that a second and more difficult poem will exist beneath it.
>
> (324)

The fact that Hemans chooses women speakers from such different times and places and then imposes similarity upon them, having them all testify to the same conventional beliefs, may well serve to confirm the idea of the essential feminine. This at least is what, in Armstrong's general conception of the double poem, the expressive or subject-centred reading would suggest. However, the fact that Hemans chooses women speakers from such different times and places and then imposes similarity upon them might also be seen to produce a certain sense of incongruity, incongruity intensified by the cumulative effect, which could equally draw attention to the psychological condition expressed as a construct. This construction is related to the external forms of culture, and not the cultures of the individual speakers but the culture of the poet, Felicia Hemans. The more analytical reading that this encourages might see the obliteration of women as individual speakers and the imposition of similarity in difference to be a strategic enactment of the way in which conventional gender ideology itself erases the identity of the woman as individual subject within society.

If such early poets as Hemans are seen to invent the dramatic monologue, then they 'invented' it to question the representation and ways of representing not the self generally but female subjectivity in particular. However, since the question of whether their dramatised speakers function to confirm or to question dominant accounts of female subjectivity is still open to debate, this is a theory I would hesitate to endorse completely. If they produce types of essential selves, then they are not, ultimately, initiating the more complex exploration of the fragmented and contextualised self that is now seen to be characteristic of the form. If the emergence of the dramatic monologue involves a challenge to the notion of the universal and autonomous self, then the Romantic women poets could be said to move towards this in refusing the externalisation of the female from the lyric centre and in showing a lack of autonomy in their female speakers, producing them not so much as autonomous selves but as subject to both internal and external forces. It could also be said, however, that the male autonomous self is thereby allowed to remain intact and the female self is ultimately reproduced in a manner familiar from traditional male representations. Furthermore, by universalising the female voice, any challenge is compromised since Hemans appears more concerned with producing an essential female alternative to the universalised male self than with critiquing, as Browning and Tennyson do, the grounds upon which that self is produced. Nevertheless, such early women poets as Hemans do produce types of the feminine against which women writers of dramatic monologues will soon begin to react. Frequently, as we will soon see, this will be done by exploiting precisely the kind of affective and expressive mode typified by Hemans while more pointedly setting it up for analysis and critique.

Finally, the important role played by gender in this theory of the emergence of the dramatic monologue prompts a reconsideration of the way gender articulated the whole field of early Victorian poetry and may have also influenced male poets to invent and develop the form. The Romantic model of the poet they inherited, as Herbert Sussman observes, 'valorized isolation from the commercial or male sphere, emotive openness and imaginative inwardness, passivity, and even the drive toward dissolution and death' (Sussman 1992: 186). As lines of gender demarcation became increasingly rigid in the early nineteenth century, poetry, particularly lyric poetry, was almost inevitably marked by the gendered division between private and public worlds. The role of poet was increasingly at odds with the new ideal of entrepreneurial manliness as it was being defined by the early Victorian middle class, with its 'emphasis on engagement in the male sphere of work, its valuing of strength and energy, and its criterion of success measured by support of a domestic establishment' (186). The result, as summarised by Dorothy Mermin, is that '[f]or the Victorians, writing poetry seemed like woman's work, even though only men were supposed to do it. ... Male Victorian poets worried that they might in effect be feminizing themselves by withdrawing into a private world' (Mermin 1986: 67). One crucial strategy for resolving this basic disjunction, Herbert Sussman argues, was to resituate the source of poetry in the attributes of entrepreneurial manhood itself, 'in commercial engagement, energetic activity, and phallic sexuality' (Sussman 1992: 187), to create a new male poetic. Gender considerations may well, then, have had some influence on the poets' rejection of the inward-looking and isolated Romantic lyric in favour of a form that placed the speaking subject so firmly within a public world. Given a form 'that plays self against context' (Tucker 1984: 127), and an age in which questions of identity were so closely implicated in definitions of masculinity and femininity, it is certainly not surprising that, as the following chapter will suggest, gender issues became central to the dramatic monologue as it developed.

4

MEN AND WOMEN

WOMEN'S VOICES

Do male and female poets conceptualise and exploit the form of the dramatic monologue differently? In 1986, when the work of recuperating forgotten and marginalised women poets was still in its early stages, Dorothy Mermin suggested that perhaps they did. Focusing on the work of Elizabeth Barrett Browning and Christina Rossetti, Mermin observed that, surprisingly, neither poet made much radical use of this form, a form that, by exploiting the problematic nature of the speaking subject, 'would therefore seem to offer an opportunity either to escape or to explore problems of gender' (Mermin 1986: 75). And when they did, she continued,

> the women's dramatic monologues are different from the men's. ... The women seem usually to sympathize with their protagonists, and neither frame them with irony as Browning does nor at least partly objectify them like Tennyson by using characters with an independent literary existence. The women did not find figures in literature or mythology or history. ... Nor do they show off their own virtuosity the way Browning does in 'My Last Duchess', for instance: we are not made aware of the poet signalling to us from behind the speaker's back. ... where men's poems have two sharply differentiated figures –

in dramatic monologues, the poet and the dramatized speaker – in women's poems the two blur together.

(75–6)

Since 1986, it has become clear that even if the dramatic monologue was not the preferred form of Barrett Browning and Rossetti, it was frequently used by other women poets. Nevertheless, a number of Mermin's observations remain applicable, with some qualifications, to many of the more recently recovered monologues. And they remain applicable, it would appear, precisely because women poets so frequently *do* appropriate the form for the purpose of exploring questions of gender.

Speakers in women's dramatic monologues

Women poets tend to use fictionalised speakers placed within contemporary society rather than figures from literature, myth or history. There are some notable exceptions, including Adah Isaacs Menken's 'Judith' (1868), Webster's 'Circe' (1870) and 'Medea in Athens' (1870), Amy Levy's 'Xantippe' (1881) and Catherine Dawson's *Sappho* (1889), over two hundred pages of dramatic monologue in which Sappho implicitly makes comparisons between her own life and the social and educational position of contemporary women. Even when they distance their monologues from Victorian society with such figures, however, women poets still tend indirectly to call forth the contemporary context. In focusing upon Circe's boredom, her longing for something to break 'the sickly sweet monotony' (32) of her restricted life on the island, for example, Webster can be seen to be obliquely commenting upon middle-class Victorian woman's existence. Similarly, in 'Xantippe' (*VWP*) Levy echoes the gendered Victorian spheres of private and public when she sets the spinning room of Xantippe and her maids against the leafy arbour in which Socrates and his friends discuss philosophy.

Mermin's observation that Barrett Browning and Rossetti tend to sympathise more with their speakers also remains applicable to other women whose monologues have been more recently recovered. This statement, however, needs more qualification. There is, to begin with, the problematic question of 'sympathy' and its dependence upon reader

esponse. Consider Menken's bloodthirsty Judith, almost slavering in
anticipation of taking the head of Holofernes and the 'wild unspeakable
oy' she will have when his blood 'courses down my bare body and dab-
les my cold feet' (*VWP2*: 50–1). For some readers Judith may well
appear sympathetic, embodying as she does the powerful and morally
authoritative voice of female defiance. For others, however, horror
might be the more predictable response to the prophetic visions of this
clear precursor of the Freudian castrating woman.

Furthermore, even if the women *are* said to sympathise more with
their speakers, this does not mean that they do not objectify them or
frame them with irony. What it *does* mean is that their ultimate target is
more the systems which produce the speakers than the speakers themselves. Webster's 'The Happiest Girl in the World' (1870) provides a
demonstration of this point. The young and naïve speaker is about to
be married and the question which initiates her musing is 'When did I
love him? How did it begin?' (35). The underlying question, however,
one she could never express, or consciously formulate, is whether she
loves him at all. Her monologue allows us to observe the process by
which she persuades herself she does love him, offering the possibility
that 'love' itself may be nothing more than a learned emotion. She has
been engaged for a week and feels herself strangely changed, but has not
yet understood this new self:

> I am so other than I was, so strange,
> Grown younger and grown older all in one;
> And I am not so sad and not so gay;
> And I think nothing, only hear him think.
>
> (15–18)

With the claim 'And I think nothing, only hear him think', the girl
appears to be producing her new strange self within the terms of
Victorian domestic ideology, with the wife intellectually submissive to
the husband. But she *is* thinking, and while many of her thoughts echo
what she has learned, others are marked by a resistance she is unwilling
or unable to recognise.

Clearly schooled in the conventions of romantic love, the girl is confused that she has experienced none of the 'flushing and paling at a

look' or 'the passionate ecstasy of meeting hands' (117–18). Nor is she experiencing sexual passion; she feels herself cold, but love, she has learned, should be fire and whirlwind. She has read the 'right' books, she is familiar with the various discourses of love. Such passionate feelings, however, are completely at odds with the childlike nature that her upbringing has produced. More <u>insidious</u> still are the social myths she has learned concerning women's roles in marriage. 'I shall be', she determines, listing a bewildering set of contradictory positions,

> ... the friend whom he will trust,
> And I shall be the child whom he will teach,
> And I shall be the servant he will praise,
> And I shall be the mistress he will love,
> And I shall be his wife.
>
> (197–201)

The persistent anaphora of the lines produces a speaker who sounds suspiciously as if she were reciting a lesson.

Indirectly, the anxieties and even the resistance of the 'happiest girl in the world' are revealed as her professions of contentment are repeatedly challenged by the language of imprisonment and helplessness. She recollects sleeping, childlike, leaning against her lover, and his pleasure in this, his resulting conviction that her display of utter trust and surrender meant she did love him utterly: 'No questionings, no regrettings but at rest' (165). This, however, is followed by a stanza full of images of transformation from freedom to captivity. She represents herself as the 'feathery wind-wafted seed / That flickered idly half a merry morn' (170–1), the words evocative of joy, lightness and beauty. These qualities seem entirely absent from her description of her coming fate, to be 'thralled into the rich life-giving earth / To root and bud and waken into leaf' (172–3). Put like this, who would not prefer to waft and flicker than to root and bud? A sense of resistance becomes even clearer as she develops the analogy with herself as the 'prisoned seed that never more shall float' (175) and 'the prisoned seed that prisoned finds its life' (178). The speaker draws her analogies from nature, but the roles she is attempting to assume are shown to be far from natural. Irony is certainly at work here in Webster's production of her naïve speaker, but her target is, ultimately, the gendered ideological constructs which repress and restrain.

THE CRITIQUE OF GENDER IDEOLOGY

As this discussion of Webster's 'The Happiest Girl in the World' already begins to suggest, the female poets who followed Landon and Hemans were far more openly contestatory with respect to gender issues than their earlier counterparts. While Landon and Hemans exploit the dramatised speaker as part of their project to emphasise the identification of the female poet with the category of the personal and to create or reaffirm social myths about the essential nature of women, later poets exploit the form to problematise or challenge conventional assumptions concerning gender. They expose the political truths behind the myths and destabilise the categories upon which gender ideology was constructed.

Inhabiting the conventional

One of the main ways in which they suggest the truths behind the myths is through inhabiting the conventional in order to expose it. The doubleness or discursive splitting so characteristic of the monologue becomes primarily the result of the speaker's internalisation of the contradictions of the social order. As the speaker gives a subjective account of his/her situation, that account is simultaneously offered for objective analysis, demonstrating and critiquing the cultural conditions which produce it. In Barrett Browning's 'Bertha in the Lane' (1844), for example, we are just as aware as we are in Robert Browning's 'My Last Duchess' of the poet signalling to the reader from behind the speaker's back. Though both the saccharine language and situation superficially set the speaker up as the type of self-abnegating woman celebrated by Hemans, analysis of her strategies indicates that she is a rather nasty piece of work, at best manipulative and at worst cruel. Nevertheless, even here the target is more the system than the speaker, and by both reproducing and critiquing the type of womanly self-sacrifice, Barrett Browning shows her to be just as much victim as persecutor.

This unnamed woman has discovered that her fiancé, Robert, prefers her younger sister, Bertha. As the monologue begins, she signals she knows exactly what Robert and Bertha have been up to by telling her sister she has just finished making her a wedding gown, and, it later transpires, a funeral shroud for herself. She asks Bertha to help her to bed and prepares to die. But not immediately. Insisting upon an intimacy from which the guilty Bertha now shrinks, she is determined to have her say. The words she pours into Bertha's ear may be sentimental, but their effect will be poisonous; she seems determined to ensure, before she dies, that her sister will be left feeling as miserable and guilty as possible.

While this may position the speaker as both aggressive and manipulative, her monologue nevertheless demonstrates her to be the product of repressive gender ideology. In accordance with the directive imposed by their dying mother, she has assumed the maternal role and this has necessitated sacrificing herself for Bertha. She has given, as she calls upon the dead mother to witness, all 'the gifts required' (39). The language of compulsion in this somewhat oxymoronic phrase suggests a telling reluctance which is further emphasised by her hesitation over the final requirement, that she relinquish 'Life itself' (42). At this point the ghostly mother appears in the room, her smile 'bright and bleak / Like cold waves' (47–8). What the mother seems to be insisting upon is silence, death without further revelation. In the chill of her mother's smile the elder sister 'cannot speak, / I sob in it, and grow weak' (48–9). Her influence must, for a time, be resisted.

What makes Barrett Browning's exploration of the relationship between the female subject and society particularly subtle is the way she shows her speaker to have internalised so much of the ideology that constrains her. At the same time as her bitterness is given indirect expression, the speaker's self-constructions serve to reproduce and therefore perpetuate the need for women's submission and self-sacrifice. She sees herself as the crocus trodden underfoot as Robert reaches for the rose, the May-bloom plucked for the merry summer-bee. And for her final performance, in a move which may well have influenced Robert Browning's 'The Bishop Orders His Tomb at Saint Praxed's Church' (1845), she creates two 'touching' tableaux as she imaginatively transforms herself into the corpse. First she is neatly set out on display in case 'any friend should come / (To see *thee*, Sweet!)' (201–2), and then she is in the grave, wearing the ring Robert gave her, with Bertha not weeping but, she urges, smiling over that grave. Individual psychology as produced by sociological conditions is Barrett Browning's primary concern, and for all the damage that will be done to Bertha, we are nevertheless not allowed to forget all the damage that has already been done to the elder sister.

The fragmented self

In using the dramatic monologue to critique gender ideology, women poets frequently make innovative use of the auditor. A common tactic in dramatic monologues is for the speaker to enact a moment of self-analysis and self-awareness through the positing of a self-image: the withered immortal of Tennyson's 'Tithonus', for example, represents himself as a 'white-hair'd shadow roaming like a dream / The ever-silent spaces of the East' (8–9), and Browning's 'Andrea del Sarto' (1855) as 'the weak-eyed bat no sun should tempt / Out of the grange' (169–70). Such self-objectification is often developed by women poets so that the self-image that is scrutinised becomes a substitute for the more conventional audience and thereby suggests the fractured female subject produced by Victorian gender ideology.

In Webster's monologues, female speakers frequently confront a mirror image in their search for an answer to the question of self. Eulalie, in 'A Castaway', after dismissing the earlier embodiment of her self inscribed within the diary, turns to her mirror as she asks of her reflection 'And what is that?' (26). The plain young girl of 'By the Looking-Glass' (1866) confronts the 'pitiless mirror' (19) hoping to see more than a socially determined 'I, I, I' (25), while Circe turns to examine her face within a pool as she asks, 'Why am I who I am?' (109). Webster's innovative use of a self-image as substitute for the more conventional auditor suggests a split resulting from the difference between the speaker's sense of self and the sense of self imposed by society, but this is never a straightforward matter of a true inner self and a false outer self. Instead, Webster is more interested in the sense of disconnection caused by the difference between what the woman feels herself to be and what society imposes upon her or mirrors back to her. What none of these speakers appear able to escape is the fact that, ultimately, their identities are socially and externally determined.

In 'Faded' (1893), the ageing woman examines a picture of the 'Fair, happy, morning, face who wast myself', asking, 'Talk with me, with this later drearier self' (7–8). Alone in the dim evening light, she hopes, the two will temporarily become one, fragmentation becoming replaced by a sense of completeness and unity, 'Elder and girl, the blossoming and the sere' becoming 'One blended, dateless, woman for an hour' (18–19). The desire to reconcile the selves, however, is a hopeless one, and the woman can only read from the image 'My lesson what I was' which means 'my lesson, bitter to learn, / Of what I cease to be' (21–3). On the one hand, she has difficulty seeing this image as her self; on the other hand, the image ironically continues to have more of a solid identity and existence than she does. Ageing women, particular unmarried ageing women, are like 'ghosts' or 'lifeless husks' (77), who have to confront 'our fact / Of nothingness' (70–1). ''Tis pity for a woman to be old' since 'Youth going', as she says, 'lessens us of more than youth' (38–9); we become 'Irretrievable bankrupts of our very selves' (69). The image itself retains more of an existence, a 'being' (137), since it can still inspire 'lingering looks' and 'tenderness' (135, 136), whereas she is ignored. So when she asks, as do so many of Webster's speakers, 'but what am I?', the answer is only 'A shadow and an echo – one that was' (135–8). The question of some inner essential self which might exist linking image and speaker is not raised; in this world, Webster seems to suggest, for a woman there is no identity apart from that provided by others, and others will only provide such validation to those with youth and beauty. The title, 'Faded', therefore refers not only to the signs of physical ageing, but also to the 'fading' away of a sense of self: 'Myself has faded from me; I am old' (36).

Marginalised voices

The majority of the women's dramatic monologues discussed so far have drawn upon the technique of inhabiting the conventional in order to expose it, and the speakers have been primarily drawn from within mainstream society. In other cases, however, women poets use the dramatic monologue as an instrument of criticism by giving a voice to marginalised figures. While with men's dramatic monologues we can observe such groupings or communities of speakers as criminals, madmen and other misfits, with women's dramatic monologues the most notable community of speakers emerges in the monologues spoken by prostitutes or fallen women, women who have been seduced and abandoned. Examples of such monologues include Dora Greenwell's 'Christina' (1851), Amy Levy's 'Magdalen' (1884), Isa Blagden's 'The Story of Two Lives' (1864), consisting of two monologues, 'His Life' and 'Her Life', and Webster's 'A Castaway'. This is a particularly important grouping of monologues since it provides a striking example of how women poets exploited the particular features of the form to dismantle, or at least destabilise, the categories upon which so much Victorian gender ideology was constructed.

Giving a voice to a prostitute or fallen woman was quite an unusual strategic intervention in the carefully managed debate over one of the predominant social issues of the age. Novelists who contributed to this debate usually focused on, and spoke out in defence of, the fallen woman. In poetry, however, the focus was frequently upon the more challenging figure of the prostitute. Until recently, however, the only dramatic monologue dealing with the issue of prostitution to be discussed by Victorian scholars was written by a male poet: Dante Gabriel Rossetti's 'Jenny' (1870). The speaker here is the male client, and whatever Rossetti is saying about prostitution, an issue which has been much debated, the prostitute herself is no more than, in the speaker's words, a 'cipher' (277). Jenny, as is usual with the auditor, has no voice, and this lack of voice is doubly emphasised as Rossetti makes a significant adjustment to the form of the monologue. Jenny is initially too tired to respond to the speaker's attempts to engage her verbally (the only kind of engagement he attempts) and eventually falls asleep. More importantly, however, although Rossetti uses a conventional speaker in his early drafts of the poem, in the final version the monologue turns, at some unspecified moment, from speech into thought. Initially, direct address suggests the monologue is spoken aloud, as, for example, when the speaker urges Jenny to take a glass of wine. By the time he observes, 'Suppose I were to think aloud, – What if to her all this were said?' (154–5), however, he has given up all attempts to engage her. There is now no possibility of any challenge from Jenny, leaving him free to speculate upon her and work through the problems she poses.

A quite different effect results when a woman poet gives the prostitute herself a voice. Prostitutes themselves did not generally speak out, and, as Christine Sutphin notes, even 'when prostitutes were quoted, as in *London Labour and the London Poor*, scholars argue about the degree to which their voices were representative and unmediated', some even dismissing such accounts of prostitution as little more than soft porn (Sutphin 2000: 511). The public and official discourse on the topic was largely produced by male writers, including W.R. Greg, William Tait and William Acton. Women, however, became increasingly involved in this discourse through reform work. In particular, they played a significant role in the campaign for the repeal of the Contagious Diseases Acts, which allowed for the forcible periodic inspection of prostitutes, and the detention of infected women. In contesting these Acts, the women reformers emphasised the social and economic causes of prostitution, a strategy which allowed them to insist upon identification and affirm solidarity. There was no 'natural' difference between pure and impure, they argued: given a certain set of social and economic circumstances, any woman might 'fall'.

Strategic identification would seem to be the primary reason for women poets choosing the form of the dramatic monologue to engage with the debate over prostitution. Dora Greenwell's 'Christina' (*VWP*) is probably the first example of such a poem. On the few occasions 'Christina' has been discussed, it has been considered little more than a conventional moral tale, marked by a strong philanthropical thrust but lacking in political analysis. The unnamed speaker tells her story to the priest attending her deathbed, and it is indeed a highly conventional and clichéd narrative: orphaned, poor and naïve, she is seduced and abandoned, and turns to prostitution. She no longer contacts her childhood friend Christina, but retains an emotional connection: 'Across the world-wide gulf betwixt us set / My soul stretched out a bridge' (105–6). She tries to link herself with Christina if only to lose 'The bitter consciousness of self, to be / Aught other e'en in thought than that I was' (110–11). When the two women finally meet, over the grave of Christina's young daughter, Christina wants her friend to return home with her, to take the place of her dead child. The speaker herself, however, rejects this solution, offering no explanation apart from the simple phrase 'This may not be' (379). Instead, acting out the conclusion to the more conventional narrative, she goes to a refuge and prepares to die.

Greenwell's very choice of the form of the dramatic monologue rather than straight narrative turns this poem into something much more than a simple didactic tale. In using the dramatic monologue, and therefore offering the speaker's words as both a subjective account of her experience and an object of analysis, she does, in effect, politicise the story by demonstrating how completely the speaker is caught up in the discourses which produce her. As Amanda Anderson has so pertinently observed of fallen women generally, the first thing that happens when a woman falls is that, 'as the phrase would have it, she loses her character'. There is 'an uncanny exactitude to the formulation: it applies not only to the woman's reputation but to her ability in any way to escape the narrative trajectory that now defines her' (Anderson 1989: 103).

The prostitute's loss of 'character' becomes even more significant when she is the speaker in a dramatic monologue, a form which focuses on the primacy of the speaking subject. In 'Christina', the speaker's inability to escape the narrative trajectory which defines her has much to do with her internalisation of conventional gender ideology. It is the prostitute who insists upon contextualising and thereby trapping her self within the conventional narrative. Christina's assertion of a 'sisterhood' which reaches across the boundaries of class and respectability is something that the speaker herself actively resists. Greenwell's dramatic monologue consequently targets not only the social and economic conditions that produce prostitution but also the underlying ideology.

The speaker's story, she tells the priest, is a 'common tale' (67), and repeatedly she assimilates herself to a narrative of which she is only one of many examples, revealing how completely she has internalised the categories of pure and fallen and how central these categories are to her self-representation. Seeing herself as a possible source of contagion, she has refused to contact Christina for fear she might 'soil' her 'whiteness' (90). Although she feels herself redeemed when they do meet, she does not accept that this could lead to a transformation in her self. She has, as she says, been 'Saved as by fire, – a brand plucked from the burning' (18). Nevertheless, while the love of both Christ and the rather too obviously named Christina allows her to be 'unconsumed' by the experience, she still considers her spirit has emerged 'shrivelled' and 'black' (21, 22). There may be an attempt by Christina to dissolve difference but the speaker herself repeatedly reinstates difference through her language, and further produces and perpetuates the mythology of the fallen woman. Rejecting Christina as sister, she instead forces her to enact overtly the more conventional role implicit throughout. Allowed to do no more than offer counsel, Christina can only echo the words of Christ to Mary Magdalene, 'Go and sin no more!' (387). By offering the speaker's subjective account of her experience as the object of analysis, Greenwell emphasises that it is not just the social and economic conditions that need to be addressed but also the ideology which perpetuates the myths.

At the same time as Greenwell suggests the insidious workings of ideology, she simultaneously subverts her speaker's rejection of the dismantling of pure and impure through the very form of the poem. Whenever a female poet uses the dramatic monologue to give a voice to a prostitute, she in some way replicates, even improves upon, the strategy of the women reformists in their affirmation of solidarity and declarations of 'sisterhood'. No matter how sympathetically a female author wrote *about* a fallen woman in fiction, the act of writing did not, in itself, challenge the basic distinction between pure and impure. A female poet who uses the dramatic monologue to write *as* a prostitute, however, inevitably complicates this distinction through the speaking 'I' of the poem. Dorothy Mermin's observation that 'where men's poems have two sharply differentiated figures – in dramatic monologues, the poet and the dramatized speaker – in women's poems the two blur together' (Mermin 1986: 76) therefore needs further consideration. On the whole, the claim does not seem to be borne out, even in the work of Barrett Browning. 'Bertha in the Lane' (1844), for example, clearly differentiates poet and speaker. When the two do seem to merge together it is a strategic move for the purposes of polemic and they merge as voices while 'two sharply differentiated figures' remain.

The disturbing of categories is even more evident in Webster's 'A Castaway'. Here the speaker's astute social and economic analysis and her comments on the inequities that cause and perpetuate prostitution appear, on the whole, to be thoroughly endorsed by the poet herself. As actual figures, therefore, reputable Webster may remain quite distinct from disreputable Eulalie, but as voices poet and speaker merge even more clearly than in the case of Greenwell's monologue. This is quite different from the universalising strategy of Hemans discussed in the previous chapter since the merging of the voices of poet and speaker here serves to challenge, rather than confirm, the conventional assumptions of gender ideology. The merging becomes particularly telling when Eulalie examines the textual traces of the 'good girl' she once was in her diary, that 'budding colourless young rose of home' (7–8). She sees nothing to link this woman with her present self: '... it seems a jest to talk of me / As if I could be one with her, of me / Who am ... me' (24–6). Speech itself breaks down with the ellipsis, emphasising a sense of fragmentation as the self is split into irreconcilable past and present selves by society's insistence on a division between pure and impure. This division is something which Eulalie, in spite of her acute social and economic analysis, appears to have internalised. At the same time as this sense of division is expressed, however, it is challenged by the very form of the poem which brings together the 'me' of the poet and the 'me' of the speaker: the pronoun may split pure and impure through past and present selves but it also merges them through the voices, if not the figures, of poet and speaker.

MEN'S VOICES

Is gender equally central to the way in which male poets conceptualise and exploit the form? In 1995 Dorothy Mermin made some adjustment to her earlier position when she considered the work of such poets as Browning, Tennyson and Arnold in '"The fruitful feud of hers and his": Sameness, Difference, and Gender in Victorian Poetry'. Although not focusing solely on the dramatic monologue, Mermin here explores some of the ways in which gender issues central to women's poetry are 'played out in the work of their male contemporaries' (Mermin 1995: 151). She moves from her initial position of seeing the women's work as somehow 'different' to recognising its centrality to the overall development of Victorian poetry. With respect to the dramatic monologue, Mermin notes that in calling attention to and problematising the status of the speaking subject, male poets also formulate the question 'surprisingly often in terms of gender' (Mermin 1995: 151). In both 'Ulysses' and 'Tithonus', Mermin argues, Tennyson demonstrates the integrity of the self 'to depend on the structure of difference created by gender' (152), and the 'two poems together represent the desire to escape the dependence of the male poetic subject on the female object, and also the dissolution of self that escape would entail' (152).

The theme of threatened masculinity that is so effectively captured by the image of the 'white-hair'd shadow' (8) Tithonus withering in the arms of Eos is also suggested by the breakdown of gendered structures of difference in Matthew Arnold's 'The Forsaken Merman' (1849). The notion of separate spheres is here reproduced within a fantasy world, as the merman who speaks longs for the return of his mortal wife, Margaret. She has deserted him and returned to the 'white-walled town' (25), to her kinsfolk who 'pray / In the little grey church on the shore' (56–7). With their children, the merman haunts the shoreline, represented here as a border which simultaneously marks and dissolves difference. Difference is marked by the merman's feelings of repulsion for town and church and by the alienation of Margaret from the undersea world, an alienation so complete that, as the merman imagines, she can no longer connect with her own children, with 'the cold strange eyes of a little Mermaiden / And the gleam of her golden hair' (106–7). This reinstatement of the characters within their 'natural' environments, however, is accompanied by the disruption of their 'natural' gender roles: difference is dissolved as conventional gender distinctions are erased. It is Margaret who has moved out into the social world while the merman remains in the 'kind sea-caves' (61) where he laments the lost days of domestic harmony when 'Once she sate with you and me, / … And the youngest sate on her knee' (50, 52).

In many of the men's dramatic monologues, it is not just the structure of difference created by the masculine and the feminine which is at issue, but also structures of difference created by the emergence of competing masculinities. As recent critical work on Victorian masculinities has shown, a multiplicity of male gender formations began to emerge in the nineteenth century, beginning with the crucial shift away from aristocratic ideals of manliness to bourgeois ideals of duty and self-regulation. The traditional male heroic figure of Tennyson's

Ulysses is set not only against the domestic figure of Penelope, but also against the new bourgeois ideal of duty and control as embodied in the son Telemachus.

In using a traditional figure of male heroism in 'Ulysses', Tennyson could be said to produce a variation on the strategy of inhabiting the conventional discussed previously with respect to women's monologues. Figures of male heroism are, indeed, used in a striking number of men's monologues which engage with questions of masculinity. Discussing 'Childe Roland to the Dark Tower Came' (1855), Isobel Armstrong has argued that Browning uses the traditional notion of the knight's quest to register a psychological violence that is 'created by a world of masculine values, of linear progress, of the goal which "proves" identity' (Armstrong 1993: 316). A similar point could be made about many of William Morris's monologues, where the brutal masculine values of the mediaeval world repeatedly lead to psychological breakdown and the disintegration of identity.

The values of the heroic male world are also questioned in Swinburne's 'Laus Veneris' (1866), where the speaker is the mediaeval Christian knight Tannhäuser. The Horsel, the enclosed and private cave of Venus, which is so 'hot' (25) and 'scented' (27), constitutes the realm of the sensual, the emotional and the beautiful. Here Tannhäuser is enclosed within a distinctly female space that is completely autonomous. His simultaneous attraction to and fear of this world is made clear by the way in which he repeatedly produces Venus as something not only seductive but deadly, violent and sadistic. She provides the body upon which Tannhäuser imprints his own anxieties in much the same way as his lips have imprinted the 'purple speck' (2) upon her neck. In contrast, there is the world outside that Tannhäuser recalls from his days when he was 'God's own knight' (209). Male and female worlds are here represented by Tannhäuser as clearly distinct, with the private world of the maidens sitting and spinning (87) set in opposition to, but dependent upon, the public world of 'beautiful mailed men' (212). Ironically, this is the world that Tannhäuser claims to be normal and healthy as he glorifies the 'clean great time of goodly fight' (212), when the 'slaying' of another man was 'a joy to see' (247). He may attempt to establish Venus and the Horsel as the site of sadistic violence, but his monologue nevertheless clearly locates such violence within the masculine values of the divided and hierarchical Christian world to which he belongs.

While what constitutes the 'masculine' is an important issue in a number of monologues, it does not seem to become the central focus of men's dramatic monologues as frequently as the feminine does with the women's. Indeed, male poets frequently seem more interested in the feminine. Masculinity is definitely *an* issue, but rarely the only, or even the primary, issue. Indeed male poets seem to find the form of the dramatic monologue more useful with respect to gender issues when they investigate the relationship of self and other.

THE GENDERED DYNAMICS OF SELF AND OTHER

With its speaking subject set against silent auditor, the dramatic monologue proved particularly suited to the exploration of the gendered dynamics of self and other. Gendered relations, as U.C. Knoepflmacher was the first to point out, were a focal concern of Browning's monologues from the start. In 'Projection and the Female Other: Romanticism, Browning, and the Victorian Dramatic Monologue' (1984), Knoepflmacher, like most critics, sees the genre in terms of a revision of Romantic strategies; this time, however, with specific reference to gender issues. In such early monologues as 'Porphyria's Lover' and 'My Last Duchess', Knoepflmacher demonstrates, Browning renders in Romantic fashion the 'appropriation of a Female Other who is portrayed as elusive and silent'. The form of the dramatic monologue, however, 'introduces a critical distance ... Browning now ironizes the act of projection by which a devouring male ego reduces that Female Other into nothingness' (Knoepflmacher 1984: 142–3). The lover converts Porphyria into an 'it' whose will is completely that of her interpreter, for example, while the duke freezes the wife who threatens his authority and then seeks a new 'object' to control. By animating these processes of deanimation, Knoepflmacher continues, Browning becomes 'abettor and accomplice, for he too flattens a female anima into a mere image, a representation, an object of art' (143). The poet is thus both critic of and participant in the process while the reader is manoeuvred into becoming 'that suppressed Other's chief ally' (143), into reanimating what has been deanimated.

In dealing with sexual relationships between men and women, therefore, dramatic monologues moved far beyond the tradition of expressiveness associated with conventional love lyrics to explore and analyse underlying motivations and the imbalances of sexual power. Swinburne's 'The Leper', for example, takes 'Porphyria's Lover' one perverse step further as he puts a macabre spin on a familiar tale of courtly love. The poor clerk who speaks has, in time-honoured fashion, loved his disdainful highborn mistress. Not, in this case, hopelessly. 'Nothing is better ... / Than love' (1–2), he declares as he begins his monologue: 'This was well seen of me and her' (3). While his celebration of love appears quite conventional, conventional understandings of what love means are challenged as soon as his declarations are put into context: 'Yet am I glad to have her dead / Here in this wretched wattled house / Where I can kiss her eyes and head' (18–20). In light of this revelation, there is something decidedly odd about the subsequent repetition of his initial declaration with the tense now changed into the present: 'Nothing is better, I well know, / Than love; ... / That is well seen of her and me' (21–4). This is one of the moments when, in Knoepflmacher's terms, the reader is manoeuvred into becoming the 'suppressed Other's chief ally' (143), into reanimating what, in this case, is no more than a rotting leprous corpse. As the speaker recalls how the woman had contracted leprosy and he had happily taken her in, descriptions of his continuing sexual attentions to the diseased and exhausted woman suggest that what this lover desired and got was simply the ability to exert his will. Even her death does not end his obsessive lovemaking; indeed, as Swinburne points out in rather painful detail, her very decay appears not to repulse but to excite the speaker:

Six months, and I sit still and hold
In two cold palms her cold two feet.
Her hair, half grey half ruined gold,
Thrills me and burns me in kissing it.

Love bites and stings me through, to see
Her keen face made of sunken bones.
Her worn-off eyelids madden me,
That once were shot with purple through.
(101–8)

Reduced to her fetishised parts, the woman appears to provide even more satisfaction than she did alive; there is no longer any risk that she will disturb the speaker's appropriating fantasies by speaking of her horror and shame.

CROSS-GENDERED MONOLOGUES

As U.C. Knoepflmacher demonstrates, after Browning ironises the male appropriation of the female other in his early work, he then moves on to the reinstatement of the female other. Sometimes, as with Lucrezia in 'Andrea del Sarto', his women resist male attempts at possession. Alternately, as in 'A Woman's Last Word' (1855), 'Any Wife to Any Husband' (1855) and 'James Lee's Wife' (1864), they are given a voice of their own. The cross-gendered monologue, which soon became a significant sub-genre, usually engages specifically with gender issues, and even when it does not, the choice to write across gender is probably never one which stands outside of gender ideology. When Tennyson uses female speakers in 'Rizpah' (1880) and 'In the Children's Hospital' (1880), for example, this appears at least partly in order to facilitate the exploration of political problems on a more personal level. Even Augusta Webster, for all her attempts to challenge conventional gender ideology, appears to have found it more appropriate to employ male speakers when addressing questions of religious doubt and artistic vocation in such monologues as 'A Preacher' (1870) and 'A Painter' (1870): such issues would not have been seen particularly compatible with the dominant Victorian views on middle-class women.

Cross-gendered monologues were produced by both male and female poets, but when it came to using this form for the specific purpose of addressing gender issues, it seems to have been a strategy of more interest to the former than the latter. When women do use male speakers to consider the question of masculine identity, it is often in a relatively straightforward parodic manner designed to expose double standards. The speaker of Elizabeth Barrett Browning's 'A Man's Requirements' (1850), for example, spends ten stanzas setting out all the ways in which the woman to whom he speaks should love *him* until finally, in the eleventh stanza:

> Thus, if thou wilt prove me, Dear,
> Woman's love no fable,
> *I* will love *thee* – half a year –
> As a man is able.

(41–4)

The monologue does not seem particularly interested in producing the illusion of a male voice and the heavy irony here would, anyway, work against any such attempt. Barrett Browning's voice comes through so clearly and insistently in this final stanza that it reinstates another version of the male–female binary which, in its more interesting manifestations, the cross-gendered monologue works to subvert.

Whether it ever completely succeeds in doing so is perhaps open to debate. The most notorious of all Victorian cross-gendered monologues is Swinburne's 'Anactoria' (1866). This is, in many ways, one of the most subversive poems of the age. But to what degree does it subvert conventional gender ideology? Sappho's passionate address to the younger woman Anactoria at the very least provides a radical rethinking of the idea of a separate woman's sphere: the direct expression of lesbian desire produces a transgressive version of the feminine to set against that established as the dominant Victorian norm. Nevertheless, in some ways it could be argued that Swinburne's use of the cross-gendered monologue reinstates one of the main tenets of Victorian gender ideology: the association of women with the body. Consider, for example, the way he interprets for Sappho one of the most conventional themes of love poetry, frustration at the otherness of the loved one:

> Ah that my mouth for Muses' milk were fed
> On the sweet blood thy sweet small wounds had bled!
> That with my tongue I felt them, and could taste
> The faint flakes from thy bosom to the waist!
> That I could drink thy veins as wine, and eat
> Thy breasts like honey! that from face to feet
> Thy body were abolished and consumed,
> And in my flesh thy very flesh entombed.

(107–14)

Clearly echoing the biblical 'Song of Songs', Swinburne strikes a direct and blasphemous hit at Christianity by exposing its underlying sadism and sexuality, but at the same time he appears to reinstate the dominant cultural position of the female subject by having Sappho vocalise desire in terms of an ecstatic vision of violent physical penetration. Women remain identified primarily with the body: Christian ideology may be challenged, but gender ideology is simultaneously confirmed. Furthermore, it might be argued, in the hands of a male Victorian poet cross-gendered verse may not so much give the silent other a voice as simply perpetuate the process of appropriation. Male translations or appropriations of such poets as Sappho, some have argued, demonstrate just one more instance of revising the woman writer into silence.

Gender as performance

The cross-gendered monologue appears to become more successfully subversive when it challenges essentialised notions of identity by drawing attention to notions of performance. 'Tired' (1870), Augusta Webster's most direct attack on the social formation of gender, is also the monologue which most directly engages with the idea that gendered identity is, in Judith Butler's term, 'performative'. As Butler explains, 'Gender ought not to be construed as a stable identity or locus of agency from which various acts follow' (Butler 1990: 140). It is 'an identity tenuously constituted in time' and instituted through 'a *stylized repetition of acts*'. The effect of gender then, 'must be understood as the mundane way in which bodily gestures, movements, and styles of various kinds constitute the illusion of an abiding gendered self' (140).

Significantly, while Webster is here using a male speaker in 'Tired', the central issue is feminine, not masculine, identity. The speaker is a liberal male who has married an uneducated young country girl, and the language of performance dominates much of his monologue as he criticises the way in which women are forced to assume 'actress parts' (368) and take on 'unwonted props' (128) in society. He had hoped that his wife, unfamiliar with such a world, would retain her more natural artless state. Madge, however, would 'do what other ladies do' (40). She has learned the accepted feminine role, and is

... prepared to talk
In the right voice for the right length of time
On anything that anybody names,
Prepared to listen with the proper calm
To any song that anybody sings.

(11–15)

He is honest enough to recognise his own fault in her transformation, admitting, 'I taught, / Or let her learn, the way to speak, to look, / To walk, to sit, to dance, to sing, to laugh' (91–3), making her into a duplicate of all the women he knows, and so, 'Whose is the blame' (125) if his wife turns from wood violet into cultivated show rose? It was he who set her 'in artificial soil' (127).

The self-satisfied liberalism of the speaker, however, is in itself soon shown to be something of a performance. His enlightened views concerning the equality of men and women become increasingly suspect as his language works more and more to separate, to set up gendered oppositions, and even ultimately to show his belief that women take so easily to their social roles not just because they are educated in a particular kind of behaviour but because there is something in their nature which makes such roles congenial, that makes them love 'that round / Of treadmill ceremonies, mimic tasks' (359). As demonstrated by his patronising treatment of Madge when she returns to the room near the end of his monologue, however, she has changed not because of any innate frivolity, but to protect herself; her feminine performance is no more than a response to the environment he has created for her.

Browning and role playing

Role playing is a central concern in many of Browning's monologues, and not just those that are cross-gendered. Sometimes, as in 'A Lover's Quarrel' (1855), it is presented quite positively, associated with the free play of the imagination, as when the speaker recalls the games he enjoyed with his lover, creating roles for each other to assume, even to the extent of exchanging gendered positions:

> Teach me to flirt a fan
> As the Spanish ladies can,
> Or I tint your lip
> With a burnt stick's tip
> And you turn into such a man!
>   (64–8)

More frequently, however, role playing in Browning's monologues involves one partner in a relationship attempting to impose a role upon the other, limiting the autonomy of the other, and often this involves conforming to conventional gendered roles.

In those cross-gendered monologues where he engages with questions of role playing, Browning usually draws upon figures that are identifiably contemporary and who could be said to belong to mainstream society; he practises, in a sense, a cross-gendered version of inhabiting the conventional. In these monologues, as 'A Woman's Last Word' best demonstrates, deciding who is being imposed upon is not always simple. Stripped almost to lyric essence, this monologue gives little away with respect to context. There has been an argument of some kind and the speaker attempts to bring it to an end. First, she encourages her husband to fulfil his conventional role:

> Be a god and hold me
> With a charm!
> Be a man and fold me
> With thine arm!
>   (21–4)

She will, in turn, act out her conventional role, moving into submission and passivity:

> Teach me, only teach, Love!
> As I ought
> I will speak thy speech, Love,
> Think thy thought –
>
> Meet, if thou require it,
> Both demands,

Laying flesh and spirit
In thy hands.
>   (25–32)

Is this, however, what he has 'required'? Is she conceding to demands he has made, or is she, by sliding into these conventional feminine roles, simultaneously imposing the masculine equivalents upon him? It is difficult to know. Anyway, this will be done tomorrow, not tonight; tonight she must be allowed to 'bury sorrow' (34):

–Must a little weep, Love,
(Foolish me!)
And so fall asleep, Love,
Loved by thee.
>   (37–40)

The language here, the repetition of 'Love' and the gesture towards childishness in the parenthesised 'Foolish me!', suggests she is already moving more deeply into the role. On the other hand, she is also retaining control. It is difficult to decide precisely who is exerting power over whom in this sexual relationship, and the problem is implicit in the very title of the monologue. Does 'A Woman's Last Word' suggest that the woman has previously attempted to assert herself in the argument and now, for the sake of peace, gives up this attempt, agreeing to submit herself to his will, to speak, from now on, only *his* speech and think *his* thought? If so, then the title is indicative of a kind of death: this is the last word she will utter burying this assertive self. Or does the title suggest she is the one who is having the last word, not only by forcing him into the conventional male role but by insisting on his silence, by persuading him to sleep, asserting that questioning and analysis are dangerous, words are 'wild' (5), and that it is better to avoid the truth, to let 'All be as before' (3)?

There is little of this ambiguity in Browning's 'Any Wife to Any Husband', where the woman who speaks desires to control her husband in ways frequently reminiscent of the more notorious duke in 'My Last Duchess'. The monologue is spoken by a woman on her deathbed who is convinced that, although their marriage has been the perfect meeting of minds and souls, as soon as she is dead her husband will betray her with another. With the phrase 'I seem to see' (43), the woman begins to construct various imagined scenarios in which her husband considers infidelity, succumbs to temptation with much elaborate self-justification, and finally erases her memory altogether. At first she coaxes and inspires him in her attempts to ensure his continuing fidelity, but the more she imagines his betrayals, the more angry she becomes: 'Love so, then, if thou wilt' (85). Love becomes something jealous and controlling, a point made even clearer when the dying wife imagines that, if he died first instead, she would be happy to take a lamp into his tomb and stay there. While he is bound to erase her image, she declares, she would spend her days impressing on her memory each look, each word of his, strengthening and affirming his identity in a defence against all change. There is something terribly stifling about all this in her willingness to bury herself in order to retain her grasp over him. And as suggested by the echo of a story told by the Latin satirical writer Petronius (d. AD 65) in his *Satyricon*, there is also something unnatural. Petronius's widow Ephesius, tempted out of her husband's tomb by the attentions of a handsome soldier, would seem to have chosen a much healthier alternative.

THE MONOLOGUE IN DIALOGUE

Emily Pfeiffer was one of a number of women poets who felt compelled to respond to Browning's 'Any Wife to Any Husband' with her own short cross-gendered monologue, 'Any Husband to Many a Wife' (*VWP*) (1889), and her response may well have been prompted by Browning's choice of title. This is the one place in the dramatic monologue where the poet could still be considered to be speaking directly to the reader, a point which may well account for the neutrality of so many monologue titles. The universalising tendency of 'Any Wife to Any Husband' suggests that the poet himself is intervening through the title to make a comment on the nature of women generally. Pfeiffer's monologue, in response, offers her sceptical assessment of male needs and demands in relationships by showing her speaker's dependence upon his wife reflecting his image back to him in a consistently flattering manner.

As the canon of dramatic monologues grows, it is beginning to look as though the form was quite frequently used as a means of entering into such dialogues with respect to gender issues, and this is an area which may well repay further exploration. Adelaide Anne Procter's version of 'A Woman's Last Word' (*VWP*) (1858) clearly engages with Browning's 1855 original of the same title, even to the extent of using an expanded version of the same stanzaic form. Tennyson's monologues, particularly 'Ulysses', provoked a number of responses. In 'Circe', for example, Webster takes for her speaker the sorceress who held Ulysses 'captive' for many years, and presents her as being just as bored by the monotony of life on her island as Tennyson's Ulysses is on Ithaca. Even more pointedly, Stephen Phillips's cross-gendered 'Penelope to Ulysses' (1897) takes particular issue with the snarling impatience of Tennyson's Ulysses at being stuck on Ithaca, 'matched with an aging wife' (3). Penelope, it is worth remembering, dutifully and faithfully waited twenty years for his return while he found various ingenious ways of putting off the inevitable moment, embarking upon various adventures and dallying with nymphs and sorceresses. Phillips's Penelope, while professing great love for her husband, seems to be putting Tennyson's Ulysses in his place as she makes it quite clear that, after so many nights spent anticipating and imagining his return, she finds him falling short of the fantasy she has entertained in his absence. 'Think not', she assures him, 'that I am cold / In passion or heart! Far otherwise' (11–12). However, his 'visible form' (20), noble as she assures him it remains, is somehow 'paler than my dream of thee' (17); indeed, it is 'but shadow of such sight' (21). Tennyson's Ulysses yearns after experience, which he metaphorically describes as an arch through which 'Gleams that untravell'd world whose margin fades / For ever and for ever when I move' and complains 'How dull it is to pause, to make an end' (20–2). In an interesting twist on this expression of his thwarted desire for continual new experience, Phillips's Penelope recalls the delights of her endless different imaginings of his return and sadly finds that 'lesser' is her husband 'returned than evermore returning' (44–5).

The dialogue taking place within monologues by male and female poets provides one of many reasons for not suggesting that their work within the genre constituted different traditions. This is an idea that, with respect to Victorian poetry generally, has perhaps inevitably been rather overstated in the process of recuperating the work of marginalised or forgotten women poets. It is a problematic move that can easily lead to the reinstatement of traditional positions or a devaluing of the women's contribution, and can even have a distorting influence on basic facts. One recent editor of an anthology of Victorian poetry exemplifies some of the dangers when he declares Augusta Webster's 'claim to poetic importance' to lie in her development of the 'womanly dramatic monologue', and maintains that she 'adapted the dramatic monologue of Tennyson and Browning to women's voices and personae' (Cunningham 2000: 768). It is not very clear what a 'womanly' dramatic monologue might be; Webster's contemporaries actually considered her work rather 'masculine' and 'virile', and she used male speakers as often as she did female.

The centrality of gender to women's use of the dramatic monologue does not place them within a 'different' tradition, I would argue, and certainly does not mean that there is any particular specimen of monologue that we might want to designate as 'womanly'. Rather, the centrality of gender confirms something that becomes increasingly clear as more women's monologues are recovered: they work primarily in that line of development which centres on social critique, and gender is an important, but not the only, focus of their critique. The polemical monologue will be considered in more detail in the next chapter as we turn to explore some of the different ways in which the self began to be placed within its historical and social context and the implication of these developments for the evolution of the dramatic monologue as a genre.

5

VICTORIAN DEVELOPMENTS

THE QUESTION OF STYLE

While the seminal monologues of Tennyson and Browning are remarkably similar in both aim and style, the two poets are usually said to have
subsequently taken quite different directions in developing the form.
Because each used the dramatic monologue in such diverse ways, however, pinpointing precisely what makes them different has proven difficult. We are perhaps on safest ground in focusing upon style. Tennyson,
who went on to use the form relatively infrequently, exploits all the
resources of poetic language. Browning, who used the form habitually,
draws upon the language and rhythms of speech. His distinctively
rough and prosodic style was not only a significant influence upon
many later practitioners of the monologue, it was also to change the
direction of poetry written in English.

The distinctive features of each poet's style are immediately apparent
in the openings of two representative monologues, Tennyson's
'Tithonus' (1842) and Browning's 'Fra Lippo Lippi' (1855). Tithonus is
the mythic figure loved by Eos, goddess of the dawn; he asks for, and is
granted, immortality, but forgets to ask for eternal youth. The monologue begins with the now ancient and withered Tithonus describing
the ongoing cycles of life and death, the natural processes from which
he is now excluded:

> The woods decay, the woods decay and fall,
> The vapors weep their burthen to the ground,
> Man comes and tills the field and lies beneath,
> And after many a summer dies the swan.
> Me only cruel immortality
> Consumes; I wither slowly in thine arms,
> Here at the quiet limit of the world,
> A white-hair'd shadow roaming like a dream
> The ever-silent spaces of the East,
> Far-folded mists, and gleaming halls of morn.
>
> (1–10)

It would be difficult to forget that what is being presented here is a poem. The imagistic, rather than the naturalistic, qualities of language are emphasised. Musical effects are created through repetition and balance, through the long vowel sounds and the frequent use of alliteration. There is a preponderance of end-stopped lines which offset the wrenching awkwardness created by the sudden enjambement and inverted syntax of 'Me only cruel Immortality / Consumes' as the mood of weariness is replaced by a plaintive expression of pain.

The opening of Browning's monologue creates a quite different effect. The painter-monk Fra Lippo has been spotted by the watch, who are supposed to arrest monks found out of the cloister at night:

> I am poor brother Lippo, by your leave!
> You need not clap your torches to my face.
> Zooks, what's to blame? you think you see a monk!
> What, it's past midnight, and you go the rounds,
> And here you catch me at an alley's end
> Where sportive ladies leave their doors ajar?
> The Carmine's my cloister: hunt it up.
>
> (1–7)

This is not what most would consider 'poetic' language. Browning uses ordinary words, appropriate to the time and place, expressed with normal syntax. The formal properties of the poem remain in place, but they are subordinated to the sense of the spoken quality of the verse descriptions are naturalistic rather than imagistic; enjambement and caesura exert pressure on the poetic rhythms; questions, exclamations and colloquialisms provide the energy and inflections of conversation.

Other differences begin to emerge from the openings of these two monologues, in, for example, the way each poet presents speaker and setting. With Browning, we are immediately immersed in a particular social environment and made aware of numerous specific details of that scene. We know the time, past midnight, and the place, an alley's end in a rather dubious neighbourhood. We know who Lippo is, a monk, and what has happened: he has been caught and challenged by the guard and there is an immediate sense of interaction between speaker and auditor. With Tithonus, it is much more difficult to orient ourselves. Where precisely would we locate the 'ever-silent spaces of the East' and the 'gleaming halls of morn'? Where is that 'quiet limit of the world' where Tithonus is doing his withering? The descriptions tell us more about Tithonus's emotional state than about the actual location. And in whose arms is he withering? Who is the auditor? To the extent that Eos has a physical presence, she appears to be as much the dawn itself as the goddess associated with the dawn.

Tennyson's more 'poetic' style may well be a function of the fact that, as Herbert Tucker argues, he in effect 'relyricized the genre, retaining the constitutive dialectic of self and context but turning it inside out'. To speak a dramatic monologue, Tucker continues, 'is normally to declare oneself in context and under the regime of circumstance', but such monologues as 'Tithonus', 'Ulysses' (1842) and 'Tiresias' (1885) 'run the contextualizing devices of the genre in reverse' (Tucker 1988: 192). With Tennyson, present context is something from which his speakers repeatedly attempt to escape.

Browning's mimetic particularity, his prosodic and colloquial language and his concern to construct a particular sense of time and place are all part of his wider interest in the specifics of the historical moment. The historical awareness which such early women poets as Hemans gesture towards, even as they cancel it through the universalising of their speakers, was to become central to the form as it developed. And it is Browning who is the poet most closely identified with the project of bringing the past to life, of interrogating both history and the historical subject.

THE HISTORICAL CONSCIOUSNESS

Browning's primary strategy in using the dramatic monologue as an instrument for bringing the past to life is explained by the poet-speaker in Book One of *The Ring and the Book* (1868–9). He 'Creates, no, but resuscitates, perhaps' (1. 719) so that 'something dead may get to live again' (1. 729):

> I can detach from me, commission forth
> Half of my soul; which in its pilgrimage
> O'er old unwandered waste ways of the world,
> May chance upon some fragment of a whole,
> Rag of flesh, scrap of bone in dim disuse,
> Smoking flax that fed fire once: prompt therein
> I enter, spark-like, put old powers to play.
>
> (1. 749–55)

Working from such fragments, Browning's metonymic imagination animates the past, using the dramatic monologue to bring the dynamic of self and context together with the wider but closely linked concern of the Victorians to locate themselves within history. This concern, as John Stuart Mill observed in his 1831 essay on the 'Spirit of the Age', was a relatively new phenomenon. While 'the idea of comparing one's own age with former ages, or with our notion of those which are to come, had occurred to philosophers', he observed, 'it never before was the dominant idea of any age' (Mill 1942: 1). It became the dominant idea precisely at that time when the traditional Christian understanding of humanity's place in the world was being challenged by discoveries within the sciences, in particular by evolutionary thought.

Estrangement and dispossession

The dramatic monologue, with its dynamic of self and context, offered a particularly useful form through which to express the resulting sense of estrangement and dispossession. This is the focal concern, for example, of what is frequently considered to be the most representative Victorian poem, Matthew Arnold's 'Dover Beach' (1867). Standing at the window on a calm moonlit night, the speaker looks out at the glimmering cliffs 'out in the tranquil bay' (5) and urges his auditor 'Come to the window, sweet is the night air!' (6). With the next word, 'Only', the sense of harmony suggested by this opening description begins to disintegrate. Prompted by the 'grating roar' of the pebbles repeatedly moved by the waves, the speaker produces a hauntingly desolate variation on the initial scene of beauty as he describes the retreat of the 'Sea of Faith' 'down the vast edges drear / And naked shingles of the world' (27–8). There is no longer any comfort to be found in nature: betrayal, treachery, deception, seem to be of its essence. That world which 'seems', as he observes with a pointed choice of verb forms, 'To lie before us like a land of dreams' (31) in fact offers 'neither joy, nor love, nor light, / Nor certitude, nor peace, nor help for pain' (33–4). Stripped of all comfort, all security, humanity is left to inhabit a world of turmoil and violence, left 'as on a darkling plain / Swept with confused alarms of struggle and flight, / Where ignorant armies clash by night' (35–7). In the face of a world which 'seems / To lie before us', the speaker can only turn to another for consolation: 'Ah, love, let us be true / To one another!' (29).

Whether 'Dover Beach' *is* a dramatic monologue, however, is a question which has been much debated. In the context of Alan Sinfield's notion of the feint, discussed in Chapter 2, the speaker veers so close to the writing poet that it would not be difficult to argue that he tumbles right back into Romantic lyric. This is by no means the case with Browning's 'Childe Roland to the Dark Tower Came' (1855), where the specific opportunities offered by the dramatic monologue are much more fully exploited in producing a sense of the alienated and dispossessed subject. In place of Arnold's eminently appropriate and comprehensible image of a 'darkling plain', Browning offers a grotesque, frightening and incomprehensible landscape, and offers no guidance as to what it might mean. With its intensely figurative language, this monologue places the reader in much the same relationship to the poem as Roland is placed to the landscape through which he travels, and the reader is consequently forced to enact much the same hopeless search for meaning.

There is a sense of present immediacy, but the speaker is recalling past events, and we are given no hint of the present context from which he speaks. Although from the very opening, 'My first thought was, he lied in every word, / That hoary cripple' (1–2), Roland appears to be telling someone his story, there seems to be no auditor. From the start, we are denied any fixed position from which to assess Roland's account of past events, and left instead only with a series of unanswerable questions: who is Roland, why does he abandon his quest, and what is the significance of the Dark Tower, which seems to be the object of that quest? It is never even clear whether the quest takes him through an actual landscape or whether this is a journey through the self. Either way, there is no sense of progress; this is a quest which seems to go nowhere: he leaves the road, crosses a plain, a river, another plain and 'just as far as ever from the end!' (157). Suspicion, fear and uncertainty dominate all his perceptions. He is convinced that the old man who gives him directions 'lied in every word' (1), but he then follows the path pointed out, and, even more confusingly, seems already to know that it leads 'Into that ominous tract which, all agree, / Hides the Dark Tower' (14–15). Fording the river, he fears setting his foot 'upon a dead man's cheek' (122) or getting his spear tangled up in a dead man's hair: 'It may have been a water-rat I speared / But, ugh! it sounded like a baby's shriek' (125–6). Repeatedly he questions the strange and grotesque landscape through which he travels, attempting to understand 'What bad use was that engine for, that wheel' (140) or 'What made those holes and rents' (69). He attempts to make sense of what he sees, 'solve it, you!' (167), but his speculations are suggestive only of his own fears; he can interpret only from within the bounds of his own paranoia. Although critics have repeatedly attempted to fix some allegorical meaning, this is something the poem strenuously resists, drawing attention instead to the very process of attempting to determine meaning in a world from which all sense of certainty and familiarity has gone.

Lines of connection

Even as such monologues as these capture the sense of dispossession and alienation felt at this moment of radical dehistoricisation, they simultaneously express the Victorians' desire to locate themselves within history. Arnold establishes points of comparison and contrast with his references to Sophocles and to the Peloponnesian wars; Browning identifies the search for meaning in terms of the quest of a mediaeval 'childe', a knight in training. For the Victorians, looking to the past was not an exercise in nostalgia but a way of establishing lines of connection. If the Romantics responded to a growing sense of alienation by seeking a new wholeness within a transcendent reality, the Victorians, in another shift away from Romantic strategies, replaced the ideal of wholeness with the concept of continuity.

Such monologues as Browning's 'Love Among the Ruins' (1855) suggest that imaginatively connecting with the past is a means of better understanding the present. The speaker here describes the ancient civilisation that once existed on the unnamed site where 'a girl with eager eyes and yellow hair' (55) waits for him. Repeatedly, that 'city great and gay' (7) with its violent past is contrasted with the present peaceful pastoral landscape and the lovers' meeting he anticipates, and he ends with the much quoted phrase: 'Love is best' (84). While on one level the monologue may suggest a simple affirmation of the value of private passion over wider human ambitions, on another level it questions that very dichotomy through establishing a relationship between past and present. This landscape not only contrasts with, but is also marked by and therefore connected with the violent past. A pastoral scene, it nevertheless does not 'even boast a tree' (13), indicative of past destruction, although now the grass, in its 'plenty and perfection' (25) suggestive of a new fertility, has overspread and hidden nearly every trace of the city. All that remains is a single little turret in which the girl waits. Here, past and present selves appear strangely fused, as the ambiguity in the syntax of the following lines suggests:

> In the turret whence the charioteers caught soul
> For the goal,
> When the king looked, where she looks now, breathless, dumb
> Till I come.
>
> (57–60)

The phrase 'breathless, dumb' becomes applicable to both dead king and live girl, and the point of making such connections becomes clear as he anticipates the meeting:

> When I do come, she will speak not, she will stand,
> Either hand
> On my shoulder, give her eyes the first embrace
> Of my face,
> Ere we rush, ere we extinguish sight and speech
> Each on each.
>
> (67–72)

The language here suggests that the lovers somehow reproduce rather than refute the violence of the past as they 'rush' to 'extinguish sight and speech'. Subjective experience seems to shut out all history, all culture, all past and present context, and suggests, Isobel Armstrong observes, that the 'will to see passion as self-sufficing is as aggressive and exclusive as the desires of the dead society for triumph and empire' (Armstrong 1993: 19). Nevertheless, she adds, this sceptical reading struggles with an affirmative reading that suggests indeed 'Love is best'. The violence of the past testifies to the need for the love of the present; simultaneously, however, in the very process of serving as its context, past violence nevertheless reveals present passion in a new light.

As Herbert Tucker has convincingly shown, Browning's interest in the past is matched by his interest in the future. His monologues, Tucker argues, 'enact the reciprocation of historicist desire, whereby the reader's backward yearning to know the past feelingly meets the historical agent's projective will to survive into the future' (Tucker 1994: 31). Browning deploys the 'trick of the poetic resurrection-man', that is, he incorporates 'into the speech of the living dead a pattern of references to the process of resuscitation itself, a pattern that evokes and proleptically figures the cooperation of poet and reader in representing the vanished past' (Tucker 1994: 31). Such a process forms the basis for 'The Bishop Orders His Tomb at St Praxed's Church' (1845), in which the bishop transforms himself, through his monologue, into a monument that will survive through time. He imagines himself reclining, surrounded by pillars of peach-blossom marble and with a large lump of lapis lazuli between his knees, on a costly marble slab, black of course, he tells his sons: 'How else / Shall ye contrast my frieze to come beneath?' (55). There is no sense of death here, no sense of change at all:

And then how I shall lie through centuries,
And hear the blessed mutter of the mass,
And see God made and eaten all day long,
And feel the steady candle-flame, and taste
Good strong thick stupefying incense smoke!

(80–4)

As the references to the senses here reveal, the bishop envisions the con-
tinuance of life through a kind of transubstantiation similar to that
associated with the mass. Thoughts of horror and decay emerge only
when he considers that his instructions might not be followed, that a
simple and less durable tomb of cheap sandstone might be substituted
for the costly materials he craves: 'Gritstone, a-crumble!', he shudders,
'Clammy squares which sweat / As if the corpse they keep were oozing
through' (116–17).

As his speakers project themselves into the future, so too does
Browning himself, and a particularly disconcerting example of the
reaching out of past poet to present reader can be found in Book One
of *The Ring and the Book*. Here Browning draws upon all the strategies
he has evolved for creating a sense of mimetic particularity and present
immediacy in his monologues; this is applied, however, not to a
speaker–auditor but to a poet–reader relationship. More a demand than
a question, the abrupt attention-grabbing opening, 'Do you see this
Ring', positions the poet-speaker talking to us. 'Do you see this square
old yellow Book' (1. 33), he continues, drawing us in even further:
'Examine it yourselves!' (1. 38), and then 'Give it me back! The thing's
restorative / I' the touch and sight' (1. 89–90). Past and present collide
as Browning creates the illusion of a tangible world in which we all exist
together.

History and narrative

The desire to establish lines of connection between historical moments
soon leads to an extension of the narrative element in the monologue,
moving the form even further away from its lyric origins. Right from
the start, there is a significant narrative element as speakers reveal the
desire to establish identity through the telling of their stories. However,

while dramatic monologues of the first part of the century focus temporally more on the moment of telling, this gradually changes. Rather than the story being interrupted by implied moments of reciprocity between speaker and auditor, as it is in Browning's 'My Last Duchess', the narrative or narratives become more distinct and separate from the moment of speaker–auditor exchange. That moment of telling usually becomes relatively static, and change, movement, is located within the narrative as narrative becomes an increasingly important element of the monologue.

The extension of the narrative element becomes particularly notable mid-century with the historical monologues of William Morris. While such a development in the form may be partly attributable to the growing cultural authority of the novel, it is also the result of Morris's particular interests. In the monologues published in *The Defence of Guenevere and Other Poems* (1858), one of Morris's main concerns is the relationship of various past moments in an individual's history to present consciousness. The extension of the narrative element reinforces the contextualisation of the self that the dramatic monologue originally effected in its transformation of lyric, locating the speakers even more clearly within a specific social and historical context. In addition, however, it also allows for a splitting within the subject as past self is set against present self.

The separation of present moment and past narrative is particularly evident in Morris's 'Concerning Geffray Teste Noire' (1858), where there are a number of key moments in time under scrutiny. The first section establishes the present context of the monologue with the speaker, John of Newcastle, telling his listener, Alleyne, of his attempts to ambush and capture the Gascon thief Geffray Teste Noire. What soon becomes more important than the attempted ambush, however, is his memories of the two skeletons they found when waiting in the woods. Within this past moment, John is prompted by his companion's recognition that one is a woman, and his question 'Didst ever see a woman's bones, my lord?' (96), to move further back into another past. He recalls the horrors he saw, at fifteen, in a burned-down church full of women's bones. As he remembers his father's hysterical response, a shout something 'Between a beast's howl and a woman's scream' (109), the breakdown of identity suggested by this description clearly registers the psychological violence which accompanies the physical violence of this brutal mediaeval world.

Lines of connection between historical moments are then established to suggest the psychological effects upon the speaker himself. John returns to the moment of ambush in the woods and the female skeleton discovered there. As he pores over the small white bones, he observes that an arrow had gone through the woman's throat and her right wrist had been broken; then, 'Their story came out clear without a flaw' (120). The historical monologue's reanimation of the past is replicated as John infers the story behind the skeletons; he produces yet another tale of ambush, which, in its connections to his own past and present experiences, is clearly a subjective reconstruction of history. What becomes particularly disturbing is the way he then resurrects the lady within his mind and inserts himself into the new scenario that he then imagines. The boundaries between past and present, reality and fantasy, give way as John, his present auditor Alleyne apparently forgotten, slips into the present tense while he addresses the woman and moves into a fantasy of love-making:

> Your long eyes where the lids seem like to drop,
> Would you not, lady, were they shut fast, feel
> Far merrier? there so high they will not stop
> They are most sly to glide forth and to steal
>
> Into my heart; *I kiss their soft lids there,*
> *And in green gardens scarce can stop my lips*
> *From wandering on your face, but that your hair*
> *Falls down and tangles me, back my face slips.*
>
> (157–64)

The fantasy of making love to the lady is marked by an underlying threat of violence which, clearly originating in John, is gradually projected more and more onto the lady, whose mouth is represented 'like a curved sword / That bites with all its edge' (173–4). Moving between the various layers of the past, real and imagined, Morris consequently draws attention not only to the ways in which past experience forms present consciousness but also to the subjective nature of all historical reconstruction.

By the end of the century, the monologue has moved even further towards narrative verse. This is a development that, Loy D. Martin suggests, may be 'an important precondition of the genre's deterioration' as the twentieth century began to show a 'distrust of sequential, cause and effect narrative as a mode of rationality in general' (Martin 1985: 219). The movement away from the dramatic and towards the narrative seems complete in the monologues of Rudyard Kipling, and can be observed in the way, for example, Kipling appropriates and develops Browning's 'The Bishop Orders His Tomb at St Praxed's Church' in his 'The "Mary Gloster"' (1894). Heavily influenced by Browning, Kipling here reproduces, in an updated form, not only the situation of the earlier poem, but also Browning's characteristically colloquial language and his rhetorical strategies, including the typically abrupt opening. A dying self-made shipowner addresses the son he sees as a complete wastrel:

> I've paid for your sickest fancies; I've humoured your crackedest whim –
> Dick, it's your daddy, dying; you've got to listen to him!
> Good for a fortnight, am I? The doctor told you? He lied.
> I shall go under by morning, and – Put that nurse outside.
>
> (1–4)

Like Browning's bishop, he is issuing instructions concerning his burial: he wants his corpse to be placed in the *Mary Gloster*, the ship named after his wife, and then that ship to be sunk in the Macassar Straits, where Mary died. What makes the two monologues quite different, however, is the extent and focus of the narrative element. Browning, as poet, looks to the past to produce his corrupt bishop as the product of an age; the spiritual disorder implicit in the conspicuous consumption of the Renaissance, however, is established primarily through the speaker's envisioning of his future. We can make inferences about the bishop's past and his relationship with the mother of his sons and with his rival Gandolf, but little is actually given away. Kipling, on the other hand, suggests the corruption of his speaker and the modern capitalist world he inhabits by looking to the past and having the shipowner tell the story of his life. While nothing is openly admitted, the means by which he became a millionaire are at least questionable. The death of is partner and rival M'Cullough, perhaps linked to Browning's Gandolf through his desire for 'cabins with marble and maple and all, / And Brussels an' Utrecht velvet, and baths and a Social Hall' (49–50), is certainly suspicious, and it is his appropriation of M'Cullough's plans that makes his fortune. While priding himself on being a self-made man, the speaker relates his past history in a way that, indirectly, repeatedly casts doubt upon his self-representations.

QUESTIONS OF EPISTEMOLOGY

The subjective nature of all historical reconstruction is emphasised by Browning when he identifies his strategy of animating the past in *The Ring and the Book*. After finding and entering some 'fragment of a whole', he suggests, what he will 'lead forth last / (By a moonrise through a ruin of a crypt)' is 'What shall be mistily seen, murmuringly heard, / Mistakenly felt' (1. 756–9). The dramatic monologue, as this suggests, not only animates, but also interrogates history and the historical subject, and the form seems particularly suited to this project. This is partly because, since it presents only a fragment in time, a part of a larger process, it is always marked by a sense of incompletion that inevitably leads to a questioning of the very process of recuperation. Moreover, by requiring the reader's active participation in the reconstruction of the past and the production of meaning, the dramatic monologue further emphasises partiality rather than coherent and absolute truth in any account of history. Inherent within the form, therefore, is the suggestion that any attempt at historical reconstruction will always be partial in both senses of the term, both incomplete and interested.

Questions of epistemology, about the way knowledge is produced and truth is known, are at the centre of *The Ring and the Book*, Browning's most extraordinary and compelling experiment with the dramatic monologue. This series of monologues is based on a collection of documents concerning a seventeenth-century Roman murder trial. The story is related by a succession of speakers, including the three main characters, various observers, lawyers and the Pope, who offer their competing analyses of the sequence of events. Count Guido stands accused of murdering his young wife, Pompilia, and cites provocation as

his defence: he had been misled about the extent of her wealth and sh
had deserted him and committed adultery with the priest Caponsacchi
Both Pompilia, speaking from her deathbed, and Caponsacchi claim
otherwise: Guido had mistreated her and the priest did no more than
help her escape. Ultimately, Guido admits both to the crime and to his
selfish amoral nature, but questions of guilt and innocence are really
beside the point; it is with the more general nature of truth that
Browning is concerned, and with the related questions of perception
interpretation and representation.

Some early critics argued that the point of having so many different
characters speak is to emphasise the relativity of perception and the dif
ficulty of establishing truth. More influentially, others have seen
Browning taking the Romantic position that art, the creative process
has the ability to lead to some transcendent truth, and that the various
monologues come together to complete a unified whole. While such
assertions as 'human speech is naught' and 'human testimony false' (12
838–9) may seem at odds with declarations that 'Truth must prevail' (1
413), these apparently contradictory claims are, in this reading, usually
reconciled with reference to a distinction between human falsehood, the
inevitable result of language, and transcendent truth, or to a distinction
between the relative nature of human truth and the absolute nature of
the divine truth. For these critics, Browning is suggesting that art, the
creative process, has the ability to lead to this transcendent truth, that
'Art may tell a truth / Obliquely' (12. 855–6). His method is considered
much like that of the speaker with whom he is often closely identified
the Pope, who must judge the case and who ultimately declares:

> Truth, nowhere, lies yet everywhere in these –
> Not absolutely in a portion, yet
> Evolvable from the whole: evolved at last
> Painfully, held tenaciously by me
>
> (10. 228–31)

Deconstructionists, who have not surprisingly recognised in Browning a
kindred spirit, have recently questioned this rather neat sewing up of
such a complex and challenging text. E. Warwick Slinn, for example
argues that 'Browning emphasizes not truth as product, but truth a

process, truth in the making, and in that process truth is both subverted by language and produced by it' (Slinn 1991: 123). The very word 'truth' is constantly subject to reformulation, to continual repetitions and reversals, and functions differently in different contexts. As we move from one monologue to another, truth is endlessly reformulated, revealing the arbitrary relationship between sign and referent. With such questions as 'Are means to the end, themselves in part the end? / Is fiction which makes fact alive, fact too?' (1. 704–5), Slinn adds, 'Browning offers the Hegelian proposition that there is no end separate from the means which produce it, no meaning outside mediation. ... Pure truth, truth outside representation, is deferred, available "some day", never "now"' (128). The Pope comes close to identifying the process in his remark about evolving truth, where he refuses to locate it in any fixed place; but his claim to have halted the process, ultimately to identify truth as being 'held tenaciously, by me' (10. 232), is not supported by the positioning of his monologue, which is succeeded, and contextualised, by two more. The process can be repeated indefinitely; as the poet/speaker suggests at the start of the last book: 'Here were the end, had anything an end' (12.1). We are then confronted by yet more texts in the form of letters and citations, and citations within citations, and the final lines resist any closure. Returning to the figure of the ring, Browning simultaneously looks back to the start of the poem and the notion of the creative process that the ring initially represents, and forward beyond the poem into other texts, to Barrett Browning's 'rare gold ring of verse' (12. 869), and to the words of the poet Nicolo Tommasei, who memorialised her verse as a golden ring to link Italy and England.

Duologues

While no other poet experimented with multiple voices in quite the same way as Browning, some used what might be called the 'duologue' in order to foreground questions of interpretation and suggest the difficulty of ever knowing the other. In a duologue, two distinct but related monologues are juxtaposed. There may be two monologues of similar length, or a primary monologue and then, separately, another, often shorter, monologue in which a second speaker interprets and comments upon the previous speaker and his or her situation. Sometimes, as in Amy Levy's 'Christopher Found' (*VWP*2) (1884), this second speaker has heard or at least read the first speaker's words; in other cases, as in Levy's 'A Minor Poet' (*VWP*) (1884), the second speaker comments upon the first speaker without being aware of what has been said. The point of the second monologue is never for its speaker to assume any role of authority, to provide any answers to the reader or to offer guidance about how to read the first speaker; rather, this additional monologue usually functions to draw our attention more closely to issues of communication and interpretation. In a complex variation on what Isobel Armstrong calls the double poem, the first speaker is subject to analysis not only by the reader but also by the second speaker, who, as his or her analysis is inevitably revealed as subjective expression, in turn becomes material for the reader's analysis.

Perhaps the most successful use of the duologue to problematise and explore questions of interpretation and communication is Augusta Webster's 'Sister Annunciata' (1866). The first monologue, 'An Anniversary', is spoken by Annunciata, who, on the anniversary of that day on which she became a bride of Christ, has been instructed by Abbess Ursula to spend the night thinking upon her past life. The second, 'Abbess Ursula's Lecture', is spoken long after Annunciata's death, as the Abbess attempts to comfort a new novice with Annunciata's story, or, at least, with her version and her interpretation of that story. This second monologue is laden with irony for the reader who has had access to Annunciata's thoughts. Ursula and the other nuns have misunderstood Annunciata and been unaware of the real nature of her suffering. To us, the signs of the psychological strain experienced by Annunciata suggest some kind of mental breakdown; to the nuns, these same signs are indications that she is becoming 'saintlier, / … growing more apart from us' (1409–10).

In her monologue, Annunciata relates how she was forced by her family to give up her lover and enter a convent. Her strict self-discipline has been a product more of her attempt to forget the man she loved and 'be another self' (192) than of any particularly strong religious feeling. Her struggles have also filled her with ambition, not just to become the next Abbess, but to become a kind of 'second founder of our sisterhood

/ Perhaps of our whole order' through imposing a 'new saintly practice' (817–18). Personal experiences, rather than making her kinder and gentler, determine her to eradicate any small pleasures from convent life, to introduce 'stricter laws' (829), to impose 'longer vigils, sharper fasts' (835), and clip the freedoms of the novices, whom she believes 'are spared too much at first, and spared too long' (840). The Abbess Ursula, however, knows nothing of all this, and her monologue reveals the process by which, though somewhat surprised and disappointed by the lack of subsequent miracles which might declare Annunciata a saint, she and the other nuns nevertheless hold her up as the exemplar of the most holy life. Ultimately, however, misinterpretation has its advantages. Believing Annunciata's deathbed expression of gratitude for her kindness to be a sign that she should extend even more sympathy to new novices, the Abbess Ursula does revitalise the sisterhood and introduce a new 'saintly practice', even if it is not precisely what Annunciata had in mind.

In 'Sister Annunciata', Webster not only demonstrates the problems of interpretation and the unreliability of historical accounts, she also exposes the process of myth-making. Much as placing the autonomous lyric self in context puts that self into question, so giving a voice to a figure from history who has been mythologised almost inevitably makes sustaining the mythology problematic. The dramatic monologue is therefore particularly well suited to exposing the means by which the self could be built, or build itself, into a myth, and to challenge and revise the resulting mythologised self. Amy Levy provides an example of this revisionary use of the dramatic monologue in 'Xantippe' (1881). Here, by putting the speaker in context, she challenges traditional representations of a woman reviled throughout history as Socrates's bad-tempered and sharp-tongued wife and suggests the possible process by which a naïve girl, eager to educate herself, might gradually be turned into a scold. In Levy's monologue, the fault is placed firmly with the 'high philosopher' who would not deign 'to stoop to touch so slight a thing / As the fine fabric of a woman's brain' (116–19). Crushing all her aspirations with his cold contempt, he prohibits her access to his male intellectual circle. All Xantippe's potential, all her creativity, consequently become poured into a stereotypically female activity as she reacts against Socrates: 'He wished a household vessel – well 'twas good,

/ For he should have it!' (237–8). She begins to spin unceasingly, until she spins away 'The soul from out my body, the high thoughts / From out my spirit; till at last I grew / As ye have known me' (246–8).

SOCIAL CRITIQUE

The tendency of dramatic monologues, no matter what their particular focus, always appears to be to question rather than to confirm. From the very start, the dramatic monologue worked to disrupt rather than consolidate authority, drawing upon speakers who are in some way alienated from, rather than representative of, their particular societies. On one level, as Webster's 'Sister Annunciata' demonstrates, this leads to a psychological exploration of abnormal mental states, to the production of assorted misfits, criminals and lunatics who attempt to impose their questionable visions and values upon the world. In such monologues poet and speaker usually stand well apart, and there is a frequent reliance on dramatic irony. On another level, as Amy Levy's 'Xantippe' shows, this leads to social critique, to an exploration of the various ways in which the world attempts to impose its questionable vision and values upon the self. In such monologues, the voices of poet and speaker may well begin to merge.

With its dynamic of self and context, the dramatic monologue is a particularly appropriate form for the purposes of social critique, and the recovery of work by 'minor' poets suggests that polemic was a much more important part of the development of the dramatic monologue than traditional criticism has recognised. Robert Buchanan, for example, exploits the dramatic monologue to analyse the conditions of the urban working class in *London Poems* (1866). He uses such unusual speakers as the title characters of 'Liz' and 'Nell', women who are, to use a now outdated phrase, living in sin, and with illegitimate children. The 'immorality' of this, however, is completely downplayed, and Buchanan instead focuses upon the way such relationships are a simple product of social conditions, the natural outcome of slum life in the city. Later in the century, John Davidson also considers the problems of poverty and urban life with 'A Loafer' (1894) and 'Thirty Bob a Week' (1894). Women poets frequently use the form to give a voice to marginalised and silenced figures in society. Ellen Johnston's 'The Last Sark' (1859) and May Kendall's 'Legend of the Crossing-Sweeper' (1894) and 'Underground. The Porter Speaks' (1894), for example, pointedly draw attention to class and economic issues. The emphasis on social critique in women's monologues is perhaps not so surprising, given that so many of the women who used the form, including Emily Pfeiffer, Constance Naden, May Kendall and Augusta Webster, were also to varying degrees social activists.

Few Victorian poets apart from Barrett Browning in 'The Runaway Slave at Pilgrim's Point', however, appear to have exploited the monologue's dynamic of self in context in order to consider issues of race and identity. Some of Rudyard Kipling's *Barrack-Room Ballads* (1892) move in this direction, but these poems are problematic not only in that they are hybrid forms, merging dramatic monologue with music hall ballad and marching song, but also in the degree to which they ultimately question or dissolve the hierarchies of race and colour. For a Kipling poem that can confidently be identified both as being a dramatic monologue and a questioning rather than a reproducing of these hierarchies, it is necessary to move into the twentieth century. Published in 1919, 'We and They' challenges definitions of difference through the voice of a child:

> Father, Mother, and Me,
> Sister and Auntie say
> All the people like us are We,
> And everyone else is They.
> And They live over the sea,
> While We live over the way,
> But – would you believe it? – They look upon We
> As only a sort of They!
>
> (1–8)

The next three stanzas become more heavily ironic as the child ponders further on this apparent paradox by juxtaposing various examples of the civilised behaviour of 'We' with the supposedly primitive behaviour of 'They'. And after each contrast is made, the child offers some version of the puzzling thought that, '(impudent heathen!) They look upon We / As a quite impossible They!' (31–2). The very simplicity of the language, the repeated use of such meaningless adjectives as 'good' and 'nice', captures not only a childlike naïvety, but also the paucity of thought underlying the almost tautological statements that are being repeated. Few writers of dramatic monologues do as much to emphasise the importance of context to the speaking subject as when Kipling has the child conclude with the puzzling thought that while many agree that

> All nice people, like Us, are We
> And everyone else is They:
> But if you cross over the sea,
> Instead of over the way,
> You may end by (think of it!) looking on We
> As only a sort of They!
>
> (27–32)

As these few examples should begin to suggest, the more we move away from seeing the dramatic monologue purely in terms of character study, and the more the canon of the dramatic monologue is expanded, the more central polemic begins to appear to the form.

Augusta Webster and the material world

The dramatic monologues of Augusta Webster (1837–94) provide the most striking example of how the central dynamic of self and context allows the form to be appropriated for the purposes of social criticism. Webster's primary concern is to question and expose the external construction of the self and to show the way in which that self is fashioned through ideology, myth and convention. Her monologues are marked by colloquial language and a tone of conversational immediacy, and in this respect she is aligned with Browning, to whom she was frequently compared. Setting her 'A Painter' (1870) alongside his 'Andrea del Sarto' (1855), however, suggests some telling modifications in Webster's use of the form. The comparison is one which she immediately invites in her opening lines: 'So, 'tis completed – not an added touch / But would do mischief – and, though so far short / Of what I aimed at, I can praise my work' (1–3).

The 'added touch' recalls Andrea unable to resist disastrously meddling with the arm in the Rafael, while 'so far short/ Of what I aimed at' resonates with Browning's doctrine of the imperfect as expressed by Andrea: 'Ah, but a man's reach should exceed his grasp, / Or what's a heaven for?' (97–8). There are other structural and thematic points of comparison which are revealing. Webster's painter is not a famed artist from the past but an unknown and unnamed Victorian 'hack'. He, like Andrea, has a wife, Ruth, to whom part of the monologue is addressed, and like Lucrezia, Ruth leaves although he asks her to stay and talk. In this case, however, there is no 'cousin' waiting outside: the lover's whistle is replaced by the more mundane summons of a crying child. The independent wife who scorns and resists her husband's attempts at control is replaced by the gentle helpmate.

Both monologues are studies of failure, but the causes of each artist's failure are tellingly distinct. With Browning the 'I' is primarily explored as subject to forces within itself, even though such forces are historically determined. With Webster, however, whose monologue is primarily concerned with social critique, the focus is much more directly upon the 'I' as subject to forces outside itself. Andrea may soothe himself with deterministic limitations in such lines as 'So free we seem, so fettered fast we are!' (51), but he has clearly had much to do with fashioning those fetters. With Webster's painter, failure can be accounted for in purely economic terms: lack of money means no training and no time to perfect his techniques. 'A man with wife and children, and no more / To give them than his hackwork brings him in', he observes, 'Must be a hack and let his masterpiece / Go to the devil' (56–9). And so he produces what he knows the critics may disdain but the public will buy: 'little dablets of a round-faced blonde / Or pretty pert brunette who drops her fan' (41–2), or pictures of the kind the public considers 'poem-like' (44), with buttercups to point up morals 'And a girl dying, crying, marrying, what you will, / With a blue-light tint about her' (52–3).

Like Andrea, he knows himself a failure, but, unlike Andrea, he takes no comfort in it. 'Come, stand there / And criticise my picture', he concludes by saying to his wife; it is a failure, 'Of course – I always fail. Yet, on the whole, / I think the world would praise it were I known' (239–42). Even this conviction that if he were 'known' he would be praised results not so much from any belief in his own unrecognised creative genius, as from his knowledge that once the critics pronounce someone 'a name', success will inevitably follow. The 'fashionable world' will fly with 'open purse' to the 'latest darling's studio and buy all, 'If he did it awake, or sleeping, or by proxy, / At equal price. What matter? There's his name!' (118–22).

The Victorian tendency to see the human personality in increasingly secular and material terms is nowhere seen quite as clearly as in the work of Webster. In 'A Painter' there is the suggestion that, as a 'name' is usually created by the critical establishment, and is not necessarily the result of any inner genius to be located within the artist, so, more generally, the self may be nothing more than the product of various material conditions. Ruth identifies the 'true' self with some unmediated inwardness, sees the true self of her husband as the potentially great artist she believes he could be. But 'who can tell', he asks, using the term as she has taught him, 'If now I ever shall become myself?' (127). Ultimately, he remains sceptical about the existence of some unrecognised but potential 'myself', for 'what is a man's self / Excepting what he is, what he has learned / And what he does?' (129–31).

Swinburne and Victorian morality

While Webster's critique focuses primarily on social and economic conditions, Algernon Charles Swinburne (1837–1909) moves more towards attacking ideological constructs, repeatedly appearing to anticipate the more modern notion that individuals are subjects because they are never outside ideology. Swinburne is undoubtedly the most polemical of all Victorian poets, and the publication of his *Poems and Ballads* (1866) produced one of the most notorious literary scandals of the age. Believing, with some justification, that the volume basically constituted a rude gesture in the direction of all the middle-class Victorian world held dear, the reviewers immediately set about expressing their outrage with a torrent of abuse. Swinburne, or Swine-born, as *Punch* memorably dubbed him (in Hyder 1970: xxii), had produced a book that was variously denounced as 'utterly revolting', 'unclean for the sake of uncleanness', 'publicly obscene' and a 'mere deification of incontinence' (in Hyder 1970: xix–xx). The volume was hastily withdrawn from publication by the reputable firm of Moxon and, after difficulties with transferring the imprint were resolved, almost as speedily reissued by the more disreputable firm of Hotten.

Swinburne's response to the critical assault was to emphasise the dramatic status of the poems. In 'Notes on Poems and Reviews' (1866) he protested in terms reminiscent of similar assertions by Browning that,

> [w]ith regard to any opinion implied or expressed throughout my book, I desire that one thing should be remembered: the book is dramatic, many-faced, multifarious; and no utterance of enjoyment or despair, belief or unbelief, can properly be assumed as the assertion of its author's personal feeling or faith. .... Byron and Shelley, speaking in their own persons, and with what sublime effect we know, openly and insultingly mocked and reviled what the English of their day held most sacred. I have not done this. I do not say that, if I chose, I would not do so to the best of my power; I do say that hitherto I have seen fit to do nothing of the kind.
>
> (in Hyder 1970: 49)

Significantly, he does not deny that he has attacked what society holds sacred, all he denies is that he has done this while speaking in his own person. Swinburne, more directly than any other poet, exploits the dramatic monologue to express all that is prohibited and attack all that is sacrosanct. Speaking in the voice of another, he challenges the prevailing discourses of power by transgressing their limits.

It is perhaps not so surprising that critics considered 'Anactoria' particularly offensive, given its transgressive and distinctly graphic descriptions of lesbian love-making. However, as Swinburne pointed out in his 'Notes', the poem on which he (loosely) bases this monologue, Sappho's 'Ode to Anactoria' (late seventh century BC), is one 'which English boys have to get by heart' (in Hyder 1970: 52). Furthermore, he asks, 'What is there now of horrible in this? the expressions of fierce fondness, the ardours of passionate despair? Are these so unnatural as to affright or disgust? Where is there an unclean detail? where an obscene allusion?' (in Hyder 1970: 53). Despite Swinburne's protestations, his monologue bears little resemblance to the translations that were memorised by schoolboys. If there *is* nothing here that could be labelled 'unclean' or 'obscene', it is an uncommonly tight squeak.

However, as Richard Sieburth has suggested, perhaps it was how it was said as much as what was said that disturbed the reviewers most. Obscenity, he observes, 'is more or less tolerated as long as it remains the specialized subterranean province of pornography; while the sacred disorders of poetry are in turn safely exiled, in Vigny's phrase, to the ivory tower'; perhaps the work was considered dangerously dirty 'not because it reads like crude smut, but precisely because its technical mastery so clearly designates it as Art with a capital A' (Sieburth 1984: 345). Unlike Webster, Swinburne does not follow Browning in reproducing the rhythms and language of speech in his monologues. Rather, more like Tennyson, he draws on the full panoply of the poetic, and his authority is suggested by his very mastery of poetic form. He refuses to segregate the high and the low.

Critics may well have equally discomfited by the way Swinburne subverts the hegemony of sense over sound. His monologues, filled with hypnotic rhythms, luxurious images, complex synaesthesia, repetitive alliteration and elaborate external and internal rhymes, appear designed to provoke not just an intellectual but also a physical response. Of 'Faustine', John Ruskin confessed that 'it made me all hot ... like pies with devil's fingers in them', and on one occasion, Swinburne's biographer Edmund Gosse reported, 'Swinburne's recitation of "Dolores" succeeded in transporting a number of Pre-Raphaelite ladies into an unmistakable state of arousal' (in Sieburth 1984: 351). Whether the ability of Swinburne's language to seduce remains intact today is something perhaps best left for readers to test for themselves.

At the time of its publication, Swinburne's language certainly contributed to making *Poems and Ballads*, in Jerome McGann's words, a 'public performance', a 'challenge to the moral authorities' (McGann 1972: 205–6). The volume actively courted controversy through its sensational transgressions, and a consideration of the intense debate it provoked suggests it had a measure of success as interventionist poetry. Some of the reviewers attempted to defuse the potentially radical effect of a Swinburne who was becoming increasingly popular with the public by trivialising the effects of the volume. John Morley, for example, talked of it being useless to 'scold' Swinburne even though he had 'revealed to the world a mind all aflame with the feverish carnality of a schoolboy over the dirtiest passages in Lemprière' (in Hyder 1970: 23).

Robert Buchanan later similarly claimed 'it was only a little mad boy letting off squibs, not a great strong man who might be really dangerous to society' (in Bristow 1987: 142). Representing Swinburne as an adolescent who would grow out of such wildness, these critics attempted to reposition the poet within mainstream society.

In emphasising the supposed 'immoral' nature of the works rather than engaging with the underlying political complexities, however, they fell into the trap that the volume itself sets up. In *Poems and Ballads*, Swinburne's sensationalism is an invitation to the critics to be indignant and horrified, and they, most gratifyingly, accept. The result, as Jerome McGann points out, is 'that they provided, by their own acts, the need and justice of Swinburne's audacity' (McGann 1972: 203). Morley may aim to present himself as the cool and disinterested critic when he dryly inquires 'whether there is really nothing in women worth singing about except "quivering flanks" and "splendid supple thighs"' (in Hyder 1970: 24). He immediately spoils the entire effect, however, placing himself firmly in the camp of the moral majority, when he asks: 'Is purity to be expunged from the catalogue of desirable qualities?' (in Hyder 1970: 24).

As Thais Morgan has well demonstrated in her analysis of contemporary responses to *Poems and Ballads* (Morgan 1988), other critics were equally concerned with Swinburne's stylistic excess and transgressions, linking them to attacks on the social system itself. There was the 'unpruned exuberance of language and imagery' which, Thomas Baynes declared in 1871 in the *Edinburgh Review*, everyone knows corresponds to 'a feverish sensuality', a 'glorification of sensual appetites and sensual indulgences'; confident that his readers will agree, Baynes warns that anyone who uses language in this way is 'dangerous ... subversive of domestic life, social order, and settled government' (in Morgan 1988: 17). For at least one of these worried critics, the very form of the dramatic monologue was a mark of depravity. In 'The Morality of Literary Art' (1867), Alexander Japp declared the poems a matter for the 'public constable', appealing for governmental intervention to suppress the 'bold and declared attack upon ideas and forms which the common sense of the mass holds to be hallowed' (in Morgan 1988: 18). Swinburne's use of the dramatic monologue, Japp pronounced, is a 'cunning trick' to deceive the naïve public. The 'confusing of ... the lyrical and the dramatic', he worried fretfully, 'has a decided tendency to pruriency and vice' (in Morgan 1988: 18). Strange sins indeed.

The generic jumble that so flustered poor Japp actually goes much further than he recognised. It is not just that Swinburne blends the lyrical and the dramatic to produce the dramatic monologue, it is that he blends them in so many different ways that critics today still often express uncertainty as to whether in fact he actually did write dramatic monologues at all, and, if he did, which of the poems in *Poems and Ballads* could legitimately be placed in such a category. Even with such monologues as 'Anactoria', spoken by the Greek poetess Sappho, the suspicion that it is *really* Swinburne speaking persists.

The speaker who celebrates an extreme pagan sensualism in opposition to the hollow Christian spirituality in 'Dolores' has frequently been conflated with Swinburne himself. Dolores, 'Our Lady of Pain', is a parodic Virgin Mary, as the subtitle 'Notre-Dame Des Sept Douleurs' immediately indicates. In the worship of Dolores, virtue and chastity are replaced by sin and lust, the passive endurance of emotional suffering by the active infliction of physical pain. The speaker, who celebrates this 'mystical rose of the mire' (21), belongs to a Christian world:

> What ailed us, O gods, to desert you
> For creeds that refuse and restrain?
> Come down and redeem us from virtue,
> Our Lady of Pain.
>
> (277–80)

Reviewers readily assumed Swinburne was advocating replacing the 'lilies and languors of virtue' (67) with 'the rapture and roses of vice' (68). But pagan sensualism, as David Riede points out, is not 'presented as an alternative to Victorian prudery and complacency ... but as a ghastly parody of it', and extreme sensualism proves, in 'Dolores' as elsewhere in the volume, as sterile and nihilistic as the hollow spiritualism to which it is opposed (Riede 1978: 59).

With respect to the notion of formal boundaries, Ekbert Faas interestingly suggests that portrayals of mental perversion were acceptable as long as they were done in the way a psychologist might hospitalise the insane for observation and treatment: 'Like Victorian asylums, dramatic monologues in this sense are a means of sequestration, particularly of their authors' own morbidities' (Faas 1988: 185). Browning, for example, plays with this very idea when he confines the disturbing thoughts of 'Porphyria's Lover' under the title 'Madhouse Cells'. But Swinburne is far more concerned to blur and blend than to sort and segregate. There are times when, as we tend to expect from a Browning monologue, there is a clear split between poet and speaker, and a sense of doubleness emerges from the disjunction between the limited understanding of the speaker and the wider awareness of the poet and the reader: the speaker's meaning can always be distinguished from the poem's meaning. Most would probably agree this to be the case, for example, with 'Laus Veneris' and 'The Leper'. At other times, as in 'Hymn to Proserpine', the poet and speaker are discrete entities, separate 'persons', but as 'voices' they share much, though not all, and could be said to begin to merge.

Where Swinburne's voice can be most clearly heard, however, is when we attend to the way in which the poems evoke their own historical moment. Context, in a Swinburne monologue, is a crucially doubled concern. The speakers themselves are usually placed within a pagan or mediaeval world, but the contemporary context is simultaneously established: the poems 'indirectly call forth the vast emptiness of social cant and commonplace moral thoughtlessness ... all the moral confusions and hypocrisies which, [Swinburne] knew, had become settled truths for most of his countrymen' (McGann 1972: 203). Some of his speakers reflect directly upon the issues, resulting in a more overtly polemical monologue; in other more ironical monologues the speaker's self-justifications function to suggest the ways in which their values and beliefs have been formed.

'Hymn to Proserpine' provides an example of the first case. The Roman pagan here speaks at the time Christianity is proclaimed the official faith in Rome, and directly analyses the icons, the beliefs and the values of Christianity. He finds them baffling, contradictory and perverse. The old gods, cruel as they may have been, at least allowed for joy. Those he calls the new gods, Christ and the Virgin, encourage nothing but grief; as he observes in one of Swinburne's most memorable lines, 'Thou has conquered, O pale Galilean; the world has grown grey from thy breath' (35). The Christian obsession with martyrdom puzzles and repels him; self-sacrifice is viewed as nothing more than sado-masochism, and he refuses to kneel to or adore the ' lips that the live blood faints in, the leavings of racks and rods! / ... ghastly glories of saints, dead limbs of gibbeted Gods!' (43–4).

'Laus Veneris' provides an example of the second case. Speaking in the voice of the mediaeval Christian knight Tannhäuser, Swinburne, as Jerome McGann observes, 'dramatically accepts the Christian perspective in order that it might be self-condemned' (McGann 1972: 255). For Swinburne, what has been primarily destructive about Christian thought is its introduction of the distinction between body and soul: it is, Tannhäuser observes in 'Laus Veneris', Christ's self-sacrifice, the shedding of his blood, 'whereat our souls were priced' (16) and, inevitably, our bodies devalued. The monologue begins where most versions of the tale end, with Tannhäuser's return to Venus in the Horsel after his futile attempt to gain absolution from the Pope. Despite his overwhelming attraction to Venus, and his ostensible rejection of Christian values, Tannhäuser is simply unable to escape the dualistic and hierarchical system of thought that separates body from spirit: it is Christian ideology, not Venus, which imprisons him. For Tannhäuser, the Horsel where he enjoys the love of Venus can only be Hell. He repeatedly represents it, therefore, in terms of heat and flames, suggesting simultaneously the flames of hell or the flames of passion; for Tannhäuser, trapped by his Christian beliefs, they are much the same thing.

Swinburne's targets of attack in *Poems and Ballads*, then, are the ideological constructs of Victorian morality, what he called in his 'Notes on Poems and Reviews' the 'overshadowing foliage of fictions' and the 'artificial network of proprieties' of his own historical moment (in Bristow 1987: 159). Using the monologue's central dynamic of self and context, he exposes contemporary society's beliefs and values as a kind of false consciousness, and, like Augusta Webster, makes the form into an effective instrument of social critique.

Into the twentieth century

As Aestheticism modulated into Decadence during the last part of the nineteenth century, there was less use of the dramatic monologue as interest in exploring states of intense self-consciousness resulted in a return to the lyric form. Nevertheless, some poets did continue to write monologues, with Rudyard Kipling, for example, escorting it well into the twentieth century. The influence of Browning on Kipling remains strong, and can emerge in some rather peculiar contexts. 'His Apologies' (1932), for example, offers a canine voice speaking to its master at various key moments in the dog's life. Starting when he is barely eight weeks old, he moves through various misdemeanours – 'Master, behold a Sinner!' – involving the defilement of 'Thy Premises' and the chewing of 'Thy Shoe', and various triumphs:

> Master, extol Thy Servant, he has met a most Worthy Foe!
> There has been fighting all over the Shop – and into the Shop also!
> Till cruel umbrellas parted the strife (or I might have been choking him yet),
> But Thy Servant has had the Time of his Life – and now shall we call on the vet?
>
> (13–16)

Dog fanciers may find the poem worth digging up and appreciate the certain comic appeal that results as Kipling reproduces Browning's typical mixing of high and low by setting biblical language against the most mundane of colloquialisms. Whether this is dogologue or just plain doggerel, however, must remain a question open to debate. On the evidence of such monologues as this, many readers might well conclude that by the early twentieth century the genre was, if not quite defunct, then in a serious state of decline.

6

MODERNISM AND ITS
AFTERMATH

THE DECLINE OF THE GENRE?

At the same time as the Aesthetes and Decadents of the late nineteenth century were turning back to lyric, the implications of the earlier poets' use of dramatic monologue were being explored and theorised by Oscar Wilde in his critical writings on the mask. Wilde saw the mask as a means of evading limitation, of allowing writers to escape both the general constraints of life and the specific restrictions of their own civilisation. 'What we call insincerity', he wrote in his 1891 essay on 'The Critic as Artist', 'is simply a method by which we can multiply our personalities' (Wilde 1989: 285). While the Victorian monologue plays with the *tension* between the voices of poet and speaker, Wilde focuses on the *connection* between writers and their various masks. As Carol Christ argues, in this respect Wilde's conception of the mask 'strikingly anticipates Modernist poetics': the Modernists take the dramatic monologue and develop from it a 'concept of voice which enables them at once to express and transcend the restriction which individual personality imposes and the historical and individual particularity which any poem possesses' (Christ 1984: 32). The movement away from the specificity characteristic of the form and the fragmentation of voice involved in this process are generally considered to lead to the disintegration of the monologue as a genre.

While Modernist writers on the whole tend to react against the Victorians, both Ezra Pound and T.S. Eliot were nevertheless influenced by the monologues of Robert Browning, admiring both Browning's use of the rhythms and language of speech and what they saw as his insights concerning human nature. As Pound admiringly observes of 'Master Bob Browning', the 'Old Hippety-Hop o' the accents', in his version of Mesmerism' (1909): 'what a sight you ha' got o' our in'ards' (7, 17, 10). The majority of Pound's monologues are found in the early volume *Personae* (1909). Like Browning, Pound tends to use historical characters as his speakers; unlike Browning, however, he frequently chooses mediaeval poets. In itself, this begins to suggest a closer connection between speaking voice and poetic voice than is found in Browning, and this connection is confirmed by Pound's comments upon his use of what he called the mask in an essay first published in 1914:

> In the 'search for oneself,' in the search for 'sincere self-expression,' one gropes, one finds some seeming verity. One says 'I am' this, that, or the other thing, and with the words scarcely uttered one ceases to be that thing. I began this search for the real in a book called *Personae*, casting off, as it were, complete masks of the self in each poem. I continued in long series of translations, which were but more elaborate masks.
>
> (Pound 1970: 85)

Pound's experiments with dramatic monologue in *Personae* are primarily the result of his concern to find an appropriate poetic voice through which to speak the self, and right from the start this 'self' is seen as something necessarily fragmented, multiple and shifting.

Although the fragmentation of voice in Pound and Eliot is most clearly evident in such works as the former's *Hugh Selwyn Mauberley* (1920) and the latter's *The Waste Land* (1922), it is something which they work towards through their earlier appropriation of the dramatic monologue, and it begins with a pointed attempt to undercut any naturalistic notion of character. Frequently, this is achieved through an intensification of the sense of the controlling hand of the poet. Pound complicates the matter of who speaks and emphasises the poet's controlling hand to the extent that he often creates the effect of two figures speaking simultaneously: the speaking 'I' is both poet and character. In 'Cino' (1909), for example, when the troubadour begins to sing of the sun, Pound appears to be singing too:

> 'Pollo Phoibee, old tin pan, you
> Glory to Zeus' aegis-day,
> Shield o'steel-blue, th' heaven o'er us
> Hath for boss thy lustre gay!
>
> (42–5)

The anachronistic idioms dotted through Cino's song explicitly draw attention to the presence of the poet, suggesting two voices who ultimately merge in the final lines of the monologue as colloquialisms give way to a moment of pure lyric.

In 'The Love Song of J. Alfred Prufrock' from *Prufrock and Other Observations* (1917), Eliot similarly makes his own voice heard through such poetic strategies as telling variations in line length and the juxtaposition of ironic rhymes. Our sense of Eliot's voice, however, is even further emphasised by the numerous references to other texts. Echoes of the Bible, Hesiod, Dante, Shakespeare, Marvell, Donne and others abound, subverting the sense of any unique or specific character and instead firmly establishing the speaker as a literary construct. The naturalistic sense of a singular character is consequently further undercut in the Modernist monologue by the highly textualised nature of the speaking voice.

The question of context in a Modernist monologue is in fact more usefully considered in terms of these other texts rather than in terms of a specific and natural setting. It is frequently difficult to determine any particular context for the speaker; rather, he or she appears to exist in an undefined and elusive space. Where, for example, do we place the speaker in Eliot's 'The Love Song of J. Alfred Prufrock'? Rather than focusing on a particular dramatic situation, there is an emphasis on what Sinfield calls moments of 'intense apprehension' (Sinfield 1977 65). In place of a naturalistic and specific setting, we are offered brief and highly evocative images. The first line of this monologue may sound entirely Browningesque, with its speaker and apparent auditor and its abrupt placement of the reader in the midst of some ongoing situation. But Browning is not so much a model here as just one of the many voices echoed by Prufrock, and his influence almost immediately starts to dissolve: 'Let us go then, you and I, / When the evening is spread out against the sky / Like a patient etherised upon a table' (1–3). Rather than being placed in some concrete context, we are immediately thrown into metaphor. We are not offered a naturalistic and specific setting but the beginnings of a process through which Eliot will create a mental landscape. In this respect, Eliot's monologue appears to be following Tennyson, in such monologues as 'Tithonus', and not Browning.

Pound's early monologues, primarily focused upon capturing mood, are even less concerned with establishing a naturalistic setting than Eliot's; indeed, there is little sense of anything external to the speaking subject. As a result, there is also little sense of any interaction with others, a trait which is, on the whole, typical of most Modernist monologues. Speakers tend to be isolated from any community, even when the convention of the auditor is used. The first line of Eliot's 'The Love Song of J. Alfred Prufrock', 'Let us go then, you and I', simultaneously draws upon and subverts the convention of the audience. There is the implication that we have both speaker and listener. But who is that 'you'? No one appears to be present. If, as is most usually assumed, Prufrock is addressing some part of himself, then Eliot would seem to use the convention only to emphasise the isolation of the speaker, his entrapment within his own mind. Prufrock has no hope that there can be any significant connection or exchange between the self and the world. Any attempt to engage with another will, he believes, inevitably lead to misunderstanding.

With Pound, there are often signals associated with the presence of an auditor, but that auditor tends to be unidentified and the convention unexploited. In 'La Fraisne', for example, when the speaker notes 'And I? I have put aside all folly and all grief' (24), and when Cino, who has 'sung women in three cities' (1), says '... eh? ... they mostly had grey eyes' (40), both the 'And I? and the 'eh?' suggest the presence of another who has asked a question. However, nothing else in the monologues suggests or exploits the presence of this other. Consequently, the convention becomes meaningless: the signs of the auditor are little more than, as Loy D. Martin observes, 'a verbal affectation' (Martin 1985: 228). Much the same, Martin also notes, can be said of the Browningesque opening of 'La Fraisne'. When Browning uses the coordinating conjunction at the beginning of 'Andrea del Sarto', 'But do not let us quarrel any more' (1), he implies a speech in process, suggests the monologue is only part of a larger exchange between Andrea and his wife. When Pound begins 'La Fraisne' with 'For I was a gaunt, grave councilor' (1), he exploits the device, but not functionally; the opening conjunction may imply a continuation with something that has gone before, but whatever precedes that 'For' is never established.

The Modernists, then, appropriate the dramatic monologue primarily for the purposes of experimenting with poetic voice. And as the conventions associated with the dramatic monologue begin to lose their functional value and the undermining of any naturalistic sense of character leads to the fragmentation of the speaking 'I', a new kind of poem begins to evolve. In *Hugh Selwyn Mauberley* (1920), Pound moves between quotation, translation and first- and third-person speech; as many critics observe, the reader is consequently faced with the constantly shifting boundaries of the speaking subject. For Carol Christ, this difficulty in itself reveals the enterprise of the poem: 'Pound presents not a distinctly delineated character but the project of imagining oneself as a character' (Christ 1984: 44). In a similar fashion, the numerous literary echoes combine with the heterogeneity of differing voices in Eliot's *The Waste Land* to erase the sense of any specific speaker. Rather than playing with the tension between the voice of poet and speaker, both Eliot and Pound can be said to create multiple fragmented voices which become a composite voice, a voice which is, ultimately, the voice of the poet.

Once the speaking 'I' has reached this stage of development, is there any future for the dramatic monologue? For Alan Sinfield in 1977, it appeared not:

> If the poet can cultivate a poetic 'I' which is sufficiently elusive and impersonal to suggest the mysterious and incalculable nature of the human psyche; which heads off the Romantic assumption that the poet's self may be encapsulated, and truth with it, in a single language act; which possesses an ironical self-awareness but does not inhibit commitment; then he will no longer need dramatic mono-

logue. He will have found his way back to the flexibility of first-person voice enjoyed before the Romantics – though not with the innocence of earlier poets. Dramatic monologue by affording scope for experiment contains within itself the means of its own redundancy.

(Sinfield 1977: 71)

After considering the Modernist developments of Pound and Eliot, discussions of the dramatic monologue consequently tend to slide to an uneasy halt. Sinfield suggests that subsequent poets either followed the Modernist example of cultivating an elusive poetic 'I' or 'strode back into the full bardic posture' (Sinfield 1977: 74). Those poets who continued to experiment with the form rarely stayed with it for long. Robert Lowell, for example, used dramatic monologue in both *Lord Weary's Castle* (1946) and *The Mills of the Kavanaughs* (1951). But as Sinfield points out, Lowell, like Eliot and Pound, used the dramatic monologue on the route to developing his own voice. In Lowell's next volume, *Life Studies* (1959), the work which first established his reputation, he rejects the fictionalised voice in favour of something far more personal; indeed, *Life Studies* is usually considered one of the texts which helped initiate the confessional school of poetry. On the whole, Sinfield observes, the dramatic monologue is subsequently put only to 'occasional use' (76).

AN ALTERNATIVE VIEW

What has been outlined so far in this chapter is the generally agreed critical position on the fate of the post-Victorian monologue. But developments in both poetic practice and literary studies since 1977 suggest this is a position which may now need to be reconsidered. The vigorous flourishing of the dramatic monologue over the past twenty or so years certainly sits oddly with the idea that the form became redundant. Is this recent flourishing, however, the sign of a revival, or did the dramatic monologue in fact survive Modernism and its aftermath in a far healthier state than is generally assumed?

A reconsideration of the fate of the monologue might begin with the recognition that earlier assessments of the decline of the monologue in the early twentieth century are based on the work of a small number of canonical and primarily male poets. The ongoing process of opening up the canon allows for an adjustment of focus which may well eventually produce a slightly different story. What might be the effect, for example, of beginning a consideration of post-Victorian monologues not with Pound or Eliot but with Charlotte Mew?

Still rarely the subject of critical attention, Mew published her first collection of poetry, *The Farmer's Bride*, in 1916, a year before Eliot's *Prufrock and Other Observations*. While Mew has usually been situated as one of the last Victorians on the few occasions her work has been discussed, this seems rather unfair given that Yeats, who was not only born four years before her but also began writing as part of the Decadent movement, should be generally accepted as Modernist. Mew's most characteristic poetic form was the dramatic monologue, and her most frequently anthologised poem, 'The Farmer's Bride', demonstrates the ways in which she typically exploited the form. This, like many of Mew's poems, is a cross-gendered monologue, and the farmer who speaks is describing his marriage to a young woman fearful of his attentions. She escapes his home, and is pursued and caught by her husband, with the help of other villagers, who 'fetched her home at last / And turned the key upon her, fast' (18–19). Thus locked in, the woman performs the household tasks required of her, 'So long as men-folk keep away', and sleeps alone up in the attic. ''Tis but a stair / Betwixt us' (43–4), says her husband.

The farmer's language clearly demonstrates his inability to see her in anything but the most conventional terms. Repeatedly, for example, he represents her in terms of nature: she is compared with a young hare, a larch tree and the first wild violets; she is something he cannot understand and cannot have. Even now, stricken by loneliness, and possibly even sympathetic to her fears, he can see her only as an object of desire; his 'stare' positions her as other, as different, producing a far greater barrier to communication than a set of wooden steps. The monologue's critique of sexual relationships attacks not so much the individual who speaks, however, as the society which produces him: he is shown to be the almost inevitable product of a set of social and cultural conditions. Those villagers who help him chase his young wife across field and town, along with the other wives who report to him on her conduct, clearly find his behaviour quite normal and the girl's behaviour as something in need of regulation.

There is no apparent auditor in this monologue, although it remains marked by the signs of communication; indeed, as in the case of Pound and Eliot, there are few actual auditors, at least ones who are living and present, in Mew's dramatic monologues generally. The convention of the auditor nevertheless remains functional since Mew's monologues so often exploit the reader's *expectation* of an auditor, and play with the fact of that auditor's absence. As Angela Leighton suggests, Mew emphasises 'the idea of missed communication, of speech which cannot overcome misunderstanding, difference, fear', so that the 'very form of the monologue becomes a sign of that alienation, that inner loneliness, which characterizes Mew's writing' (Leighton *VWP*: 646). In the hands of Charlotte Mew, then, the Modernist monologue can be characterised as a form which continued to be appropriated for the purposes of social critique and which was considered to be particularly well suited to the exploration of the issues of representation and communication.

Much the same conclusion might be reached if the grouping of dramatic monologues is expanded to include the work of non-canonical poets from the following decades, particularly if we incorporate the overtly politicised voices of such black American poets as Langston Hughes and Gwendolyn Brooks. Eliot and Pound cultivated an 'elusive and impersonal voice' which could suggest the 'mysterious and incalculable nature of the human psyche' (Sinfield 1977: 71), and they aimed to transcend 'historical and individual particularity' (Christ 1984: 32). Such a voice may not have appeared particularly congenial to poets such as Hughes and Brooks, for whom identity was still something which needed to be claimed and established; these poets appear to have found the original form of far more use for their particular purposes. Like Mew, they appropriated the dramatic monologue primarily for social critique, and the emphasis in their monologues is on the questions of representation and communication.

At a time when poetic language was increasingly formal and literary, characterised by finely crafted and complex sentences or, if it veered more towards the informal and conversational, by the educated idiom of the middle class, Langston Hughes was revitalising the dramatic monologue through the introduction of the idioms of black folk speech and street talk. He frequently speaks in the voice of a black woman, and while some of these speakers lean towards the representative, others are highly individualised, particularly when the focus is the assertion of control over one's identity. In *Madam to You: The Life and Times of Alberta K. Johnson* (Part I of *One-Way Ticket*, 1949), for example Hughes produces a series of twelve monologues, all spoken by Alberta K. Johnson, but in different contexts and with different auditors. Many of these monologues focus upon questions of representation and communication. In 'Madam and the Census Man', for example, Madam resists any tampering with her identity when the census man queries and ridicules the 'K' in her name, unaware of black naming tradition and wanting to turn it into 'Kay'. In 'Madam's Calling Cards' misunderstanding is caused by a confusion over terminology as the printer suggests either Roman or Old English typeface and Madam insists that American is best. Throughout the sequence, and particularly in such monologues as 'Madam and her Madam', and 'Madam and the Rent Man', Hughes critiques the system as Madam resists exploitation and exposes the conditions of black urban life.

Gwendolyn Brooks similarly frequently appropriates the monologue for the purposes of social critique. ' "Negro" Hero' (1945), for example gives a voice to a black soldier in World War II and, by establishing the connection between war and racism, investigates and interrogates racial politics in America. As the subtitle explains, the monologue is based on the experiences of Dorie Miller, a black soldier serving aboard the US *West Virginia* when it was docked at Pearl Harbor and the ship was attacked by Japanese aircraft. Miller, a messman confined to the galley defied regulations to come up on deck, manned a machine gun and destroyed two of the attacking aircraft. He was awarded the Navy Cross for Bravery but promoted only to Mess Attendant First Class. The monologue problematises both the idea of the enemy's identity and the focus of the battle in a war which, while supposedly fought to contest a racist ideology, in fact perpetrated racism by denying blacks both combat roles and leadership positions.

It may well be, then, that the dramatic monologue survived Modernism and its aftermath in a more vigorous state than is generally believed, and that it survived primarily as an instrument of social critique. And if we look again at some of the poets more usually cited as examples of twentieth-century practitioners of the monologue by such critics as Alan Sinfield and Elizabeth Howe, it is interesting to see how frequently the works mentioned are in fact polemical. In 'Mr Edwards and the Spider' (1946), for example, Robert Lowell uses dramatic monologue for the purposes of critiquing Calvinism and rejecting his New England heritage. Edgar Lee Masters's *Spoon River Anthology* (1916), a series of 244 monologues spoken by the graveyard dead to a variety of different living auditors, addresses such issues as political corruption and the effects of industrialism. Nevertheless, while the expansion of the canon may suggest that the form did not become redundant, it was admittedly no longer as popular as it had been with the Victorians and was not the primary choice of any particular poet. By the late 1960s, however, there are clear signs of a growing revival of interest in the form. Two poets who began to use the dramatic monologue regularly, Richard Howard in America and Edwin Morgan in Scotland, provide useful examples of how the opportunities presented by the form began to be more fully exploited at this time.

SIXTIES REVIVAL

On the surface, Richard Howard and Edwin Morgan might seem to have little in common. While both frequently use the dramatic monologue, Howard remains, formally, relatively conservative and traditional while Morgan is highly experimental. In two important ways, however, these poets are closely connected. First, each uses the monologue primarily to engage with the issue of communication. Second, while many of their contemporaries were reinstating the idea of an authoritative speaking self, each poet instead questioned this authoritative self by drawing attention to the processes by which the self was constructed and thereby emphasising the question of representation. It may also be worth noting that both of these poets are also translators, another version of speaking in another's voice.

Howard's monologues are strongly influenced by Browning, an influence that is clear from the start of his collection *Untitled Subjects* (1969) when he speaks on the dedication page of 'the great poet of otherness ... who said, as I should like to say, "I'll tell my tale as though 'twere none of mine." ' Like Browning and William Morris, Howard uses the monologue primarily to engage with and to interrogate history and the historical subject. His concern with the historical moment is emphasised by the very titles of his monologues. While Browning tends either to name or at least to gesture towards the identity of his speaking subjects in his titles, as in 'Andrea del Sarto' or 'My Last Duchess', Howard's historical speakers are, as the title of the collection indicates, untitled subjects. The identities of his speakers, who include Sir Walter Scott, John Ruskin and Richard Strauss, are usually fixed by date, by a moment in history, starting in 1801 and ending in 1915. Further information about the speakers is given only in a series of notes at the start of the volume. In itself, this begins to suggest that these speaking subjects are no more than the product of particular historical moments.

Each speaker is not only a subject of history but also subject to history, to both past and future, and to the very processes of reconstructing the historical self. This is something of which the speakers are fully aware. The monologues are both based upon and full of references to memoirs, diaries and letters. Each speaker is concerned either to recover or to save and thereby write history in his or her attempt to consolidate identity and communicate the self to the other. The implication is that they fail, or, at the very most, their efforts are a qualified success. Repeatedly, the possibility of misrepresentation or misinterpretation is suggested and the viability of various methods of preservation is questioned. Supposedly more authoritative records of history are seen as no more reliable than these personal records. As observed by the rector of Boulge, who speaks in '1852', the very process of turning the past into history through writing turns the past into a novel: as soon as it is written down as history it inevitably becomes fiction, becoming misrepresentative in the very process of selecting the scenes.

This is particularly well demonstrated by the last monologue in the collection, '1915: A Pre-Raphaelite Ending, London'. The speaker is Jane Morris, wife of William Morris but also the lover of Dante Gabriel Rossetti and the model for many of Rossetti's paintings. The monologue opens with Jane addressing her daughter, May, who is unpacking for her a box full of memories. As May takes out photographs, letters and drawings, Jane is prompted to some recollection and in the process some basic story of her life is established out of the jumble of memories. Her life, her very self, becomes no more than the product of these 'things'. But how accurate is the 'history' we can deduce from this monologue, and how reliable are the representations of the selves which are produced?

In the very act of producing history, Howard suggests throughout *Untitled Subjects*, the past is misrepresented and parts of it erased, and this has significant implications for the speaking subject. In 'A Pre-Raphaelite Ending' Howard himself contributes to the process of distortion from the very moment he identifies his speaker by date. The monologue is set in 1915; Jane actually died early in 1914, at the age of seventy-five. And she died before the outbreak of World War I, although here she is shown worrying about the Zeppelins used to bomb London. Quotations abound, as Jane remembers what someone said or has May read out from a letter; however, while some of these quotations are correctly attributed and placed within the correct context, others are misattributed and placed in different contexts. Words from a letter Ruskin wrote to Swinburne after reading *Poems and Ballads*, for example – 'I should as soon try / finding fault with him / as with a nightshade blossom' (106–8) – are here said to be written by Ruskin upon a sealed envelope containing drawings of Jane by Rossetti. Similarly, words actually spoken by Swinburne are attributed to William Morris on his deathbed: ' "The clothes are well enough," were his last words, / "but where has the body gone?" ' (204–5). As Jane herself attempts to reconstruct moments from the past, the possibility of error, of misrepresentation, is a constant concern. At one point she recalls William in a rage asking

> ... 'Is it
> nothing but make-believe, am I no more
> than Louis XVI
> tinkering with locks?
>
> ...
>
> tinkering with locks, and too late ...'
> With locks, did he say,
> or clocks? Clocks, I think.

$$(51–60)$$

It is Jane who is preoccupied here with clocks, with time, and her own concerns which shape the past and with it her husband.

Nevertheless, while Jane's perceptions can be said to shape the past and the figures from her past, she herself remains an elusive figure. So much of her reconstruction is based on giving a voice to the various men in her life that the one thing ultimately erased by her attempts to recover and save her past is her self. 'I speak of my own life' (63), she says at one point, but little is communicated about her 'own life'. She sees herself purely in terms of her relationships with others, and indeed she suggests this is all a woman has:

> ... She
> stays at home, the man goes forth. A husband's
> absence, a daughter's
> anger, a lover's
> suspicion – that is her lot.
>
> (63–7)

It could be argued that Howard himself, while establishing Jane as historical subject by giving her a voice, is nevertheless still contributing to her erasure as subject by seeing her primarily in her relationships with the men of the Pre-Raphaelite movement. So many other voices, those of Morris, Rossetti, Ruskin and others, surface in Jane's monologue that at times they almost drown out her own. On the other hand, it could be said that Howard is drawing attention to the process by which she came to be, and continues to be, erased as a subject through history. While some feminist historians have attempted to recover Jane's own story and to emphasise her own contributions to the Pre-Raphaelite movement, she has come to be more generally known only in relation to the male poets and artists of the movement. In the popular imagination, she is reduced to one of the 'mere images' that in her final lines she rejects, a Persephone on a poster, 'wonderful but dead'. Even Jane can think of herself only through such representations, describing herself, for example, like Mariana in the moated grange. The 'things' she wants May to save, as the final lines make clear, constitute what she is, are a means of saving herself: 'These are mine. Save them. / I have nothing save them' (212–13). But since these things that define her are ultimately only memories of others, it is these things that ultimately also erase her.

While Richard Howard has continued to produce relatively traditional versions of the dramatic monologue, Edwin Morgan has been, as with all the poetic forms he exploits, highly experimental, and he gives voices to a strange array of creatures and objects as well as people. These dramatic monologues often function to introduce unfamiliar perspectives on human experience or to problematise questions of communication. There are clear signs of an attempt to communicate in 'The Loch Ness Monster' (1968), even given the difficulties posed by the speaker's language. It is not all that difficult to deduce that the monster who splutters 'Splgraw fok fok splgrafhatchgabrlgabrl fok splfok / Zgra kra gka fok!' (7–8) has simply lost all patience, or, given the hordes of vistors who descend upon Loch Ness each year, to imagine to whom his splutterings are addressed. The dolphin in 'The Dolphin's Song' (1970) talks of humouring man, who is 'a fool / as a rule' (1–2) and so far 'only plays with hoops' even though 'we suspect he talks' (4–5). There is no sense of an auditor here, and neither is the monologue marked by those signs of attempted communication that we expect to find in a monologue, but this appears to be part of the point: 'really', the dolphin observes, 'we must try to communicate / before it is too late' (8–9). Communication in our technological world becomes the issue in 'The Computer's First Christmas Card' (1968) when after many attempts the 'speaker' at least finally manages 'MERRYCHR/YSANTHEMUM' (34–5). 'Hyena' (1973) comes closer to a more conventional monologue with respect to communication, since the animal is speaking directly to a 'you'. Pointing forward to the way in which the addressed 'you' will be transformed in many contemporary monologues, however, the 'you' to whom the hyena speaks seems to be not an auditor within the poem but the reader outside the poem.

Perhaps Morgan's most interesting experiment with the monologue, and the poem upon which I want to focus, is 'Message Clear' (1968). Morgan here questions the stability of any representation of the self and problematises issues of communication at the same time as he pushes the form to its generic limits. Dramatic monologue here meets concrete poem, and the 'I' that is put into question is, in Coleridge's terms, the infinite I Am': the speaker, as Morgan has suggested, is supposed to be Christ on the cross (in Gregson 1996: 135). Fifty-five lines are arranged in a long column on the page, creating the shape of the 'I' itself. The entire poem, however, is produced out of one line drawn from the gospel of St John: 'I am the resurrection and the life' (John 11.25). This 'message' is only given in full, only becomes 'clear', in the very last line. Within the other fifty-four lines, the phrase is defamiliarised, parts of it omitted as it is broken down into separate words, parts of words, and individual letters. Letters appear within a line only in the same position as they appear in the final line, gesturing towards some kind of stability and continuity. This is repeatedly undercut, however, by the way in which different letters are omitted in each line, resulting in both a continual variation in the placement and length of spaces, and in a wide variety of different potential messages. The kind of defamiliarisation in question here is a development on the specific techniques of estrangement associated with the Russian Formalist critics of the early twentieth century, whereby under the pressure of literary devices ordinary language is made strange and, in the process, so too is the everyday world.

Although supposed to be spoken by Christ on the cross, a moment associated with hesitation and doubt, the original context in which the line is spoken in the gospel of St John is one of unassailable faith, confidence and power. It is Christ's declaration to Martha just before he raises Lazarus from the dead. This, then, is the 'I' of ultimate authority, the 'I' with the power of life and death. Here, however, the control, the confidence and the authority of that ultimate 'I' are questioned by the text in two main ways. First, the placement of words, letters and spaces conveys, as Roderick Watson observes, 'a remarkably powerful sense of hesitation and even deep self-doubt' (Watson 1997: 175). This is something difficult to recognise if the lines are simply reproduced with the words reconstructed and spaces eliminated: 'am i / if / i am he / hero /hurt /there and/ here and /here/ and / there' (1–8). The hesitation, doubt and resistance of the lines only emerge when we see them as they are reproduced upon the page.

```
    am              i
                            if
    i am                    he
        he r        o
        h    ur   t
        the re          and
        he      re      and
        he re
```

The opening immediately selects letters from the full line to turn assertion into question, then to a tentative admission of possibility, only to break down identity as it becomes unclear whether we should read 'he her o hurt' or 'he hero hurt'.

As this last point of confusion suggests, the need for the reader's active participation in interpretation characteristic of the dramatic monologue is radically intensified by this concrete poem. It is difficult to be sure what is being said. The breaking down of the words, the destabilisation of the authoritative statement, allows for the introduction of other possible and sometimes contradictory meanings, other messages, even other identities:

```
i am the   sur          d
...
i am th            o        th
i am     r              a
i am the   su      n
```

$$(25, 34-6)$$

A 'surd' is either an irrational quantity in mathematics or a voiceless consonant; Thoth is the ancient Egyptian ibis-headed god of art and science, and Ra the Egyptian sun god. Clearly, this is no longer a god who can confidently declare 'I am that I am' (Exodus 3.14).

Such a destabilisation of the self is effected in many of Morgan's other monologues, and explored in the most literal manner possible by 'In Sobieski's Shield' (1968). Earth has been destroyed by 'solar withdrawal', and the speaker and his family have escaped since they were dematerialised the day before, literally broken down into their components, and then reassembled on a small planet, 'in our right mind', the speaker hopes, 'approximately though not unshaken and admittedly / not precisely those who set out' (9–11). Written at a time of particular interest in space travel, 'In Sobieski's Shield' also demonstrates another feature typical of many of Morgan's monologues: his focus upon events of contemporary relevance. In 'Stobhill' (1973), for example, Morgan develops the strategy used by Browning in *The Ring and the Book* and offers different perspectives on a single event to problematise questions of interpretation and communication. Unlike

Browning, however, who looks to the historical past, Morgan draws upon an event widely publicised by the contemporary media: a seven months baby was aborted and the foetus, placed by a doctor into a paper disposal bag and sent via a porter to be burned in the incinerator, was found by the boilerman to be alive. The poem consists of five monologues, 'The Doctor', 'The Boilerman', 'The Mother', 'The Father' and 'The Porter', and each speaker tells his or her side of the events, complicating the issue of blame and leading to a questioning of the wider underlying social issues. Morgan also offers a particularly contemporary take on the monologue's dynamic of self and context in the more recent twenty-seven monologues of *From the Video Box* (1986). Based upon an actual experiment with booths set up in Glasgow, the speakers have entered a 'video box' to record their responses to what they have seen on television. In responding so directly to contemporary events and concerns through his dramatic monologues, Morgan, as the next chapter will demonstrate, anticipates one of the main strategies drawn upon by those contemporary poets who have more recently begun to appropriate and exploit this poetic form.

7

CONTEMPORARY DRAMATIC MONOLOGUES

THE DRAMATIC MONOLOGUE AND SOCIETY

In Britain, the first years of the new millennium have appeared to suggest that we are living in an age far more conducive to the flourishing of lyric than of dramatic monologue. In Edinburgh, the Fringe Festival of 2001 was dominated by the personal and the confessional, from the New York grandmother who talked about her sex life to the Bradford teacher who spoke of her brush with cancer. Television increasingly invites us to peruse the most intimate details of 'real' lives. Indeed, the very art of fiction, suggested the novelist A.L. Kennedy in an address at the Edinburgh Book Festival, is threatened by the growing vogue for the personal and the culture of de-fictionalisation driven partly by the mania for reality TV (reported in *The Guardian*, Monday, 13 August 2001: A.5). The continuing prioritising of the individual and the personal suggests we are still living in a world where, as Margaret Thatcher so notoriously proclaimed, 'there is no such thing as society'. And this vogue for the personal seems to be a particularly virulent virus, infecting, for example, even Japan, a country not perceived by the West as being particularly associated with rampant individualism. When the Japanese post office experimented with allowing people to put pictures of themselves on postage stamps, the idea proved so popular that huge queues formed in the early hours of the morning, and the special sheets prepared for the promotion quickly ran out (reported in *The Guardian Weekend*, 11 August 2001: 7). Indeed, the widespread commodification of personality and authenticity over the past twenty years might lead to the expectation that the poetry market would have been saturated with nothing more than endless variations of Walt Whitman's 'Song of Myself'.

And yet the dramatic monologue, with its fictionalised voice and its central dynamic of self and other, has not only survived but has undergone a significant resurgence of popularity during this time. A variety of related factors appear to be implicated in this revival of interest. To begin with, the dramatic monologue is now considered a particularly accessible form, and its conventions have become increasingly familiar to a wide audience. The readers of Browning and Tennyson's original dramatic monologues, faced with a radically new genre, were left bewildered. Today, the editors of *The New Poetry* can justifiably claim of Carol Ann Duffy that it is her habitual use of dramatic monologue that enables her 'to popularise complex ideas about language and its political role and meanings' (Hulse *et al.* 1993: 17).

But why should the dramatic monologue now be considered a widely accessible form? It may have something to do with its close interrelationship with other more popular genres and the ways in which its techniques and conventions appear to have spilled over into various other media forms. Comedians, for example, frequently assume the role of a character, fictional or otherwise. Sometimes this involves the development of a particular persona over an extended period of time, as in the case of, for example, Woody Allen, and then the speaking persona tends to become conflated with the comedian, moving the feint away from the fictional. At other times, however, a more distinct split between the comedian and the persona is maintained, as in the case of the monologues of Bob Newhart and Joyce Grenfell, or, more recently, the BBC2 television series *Marion & Geoff* (2001, 2003).

Theatrical monologues have also often developed in a way that interrelates with the form of poetic monologue. In America this has been particularly notable in the case of Anna Deavere Smith's performance art. Smith interviews individuals who have been in some way involved in a crisis of national import and edits their words to produce a series of monologues. In *Twilight: Los Angeles, 1992* (1992), for example, she assumes the personae of a variety of people involved in or touched by the riots which broke out after a jury acquitted four police officers of the beating of a black suspect, Rodney King. She becomes, in turn, such characters as a Hollywood talent agent who hid in a hotel, a Korean grocer who protected his shop from his rooftop with a gun, a gang member, and the police chief who dallied at a fund-raising event as the city burned. By having all these people speak in turn on the same issue, Smith could be seen as producing a theatrical late twentieth-century version of Browning's *The Ring and the Book*. Eve Ensler's *The Vagina Monologues* (1996) are similarly based upon a series of actual interviews. In Britain, Alan Bennett's *Talking Heads* provides another demonstration of the interaction of the genres of poetic and theatrical monologue. These monologues, performed originally on television (1988) and subsequently in the theatre (1992), in many ways resemble Browning's most ironic pieces, and Bennett himself has spoken of them in much the same terms as early critics spoke of Browning's monologues. Describing the speakers as 'artless', he observes that '[t]hey didn't quite know what they are saying and are telling a story to the meaning of which they are not entirely privy' (Bennett 1987: 7).

Song lyrics provide yet one more example of how the conventions of the dramatic monologue have spilled over into other genres. In this context it is perhaps worth noting that Robert Langbaum, in his seminal *The Poetry of Experience*, originally suggested this connection by comparing the apparently spontaneous outpouring of the dramatic monologue to breaking out in song (Langbaum 1957: 183). Numerous examples of song lyrics reminiscent of dramatic monologues could be cited, from such blues and jazz lyrics as Otis Redding's 'Dock of the Bay' (1967) to contemporary rap music. Country music, while it sometimes tends more to the narrative than the dramatic, offers many examples of lyrics which resemble dramatic monologues, from Tammy Wynette's 'D.I.V.O.R.C.E.' (1968) to Brad Paisley's more recent 'Me Neither' (1999). Both of these song lyrics would even probably fulfil most of the requirements of Ina Beth Sessions as set down in her early taxonomic article on the dramatic monologue. The lyrics of Bruce Springsteen's songs demonstrate how the conventions of dramatic monologue have been appropriated for the purposes of serious social critique. While Springsteen is most frequently associated with the projection of the voice of the alienated working man, many of his speakers are in fact far more individualised than this. In the title song of *Nebraska* (1982), for example, Springsteen assumes the voice of the serial killer Charles Starkweather, at the moment just before he is going to be electrocuted. More recently, in *The Rising* (2002), written in response to the events of 11 September 2001, Springsteen adopts a number of personae, including, in 'Paradise', that of a Middle Eastern suicide bomber. Steve Earle similarly speaks in the voice of a terrorist in 'John Walker's Blues' from his album *Jerusalem*, but here, much more controversially, the speaker is not a generalised terrorist but a convicted American Taliban conscript.

A wide variety of different monologues can therefore be heard in contemporary society, and while they may well belong, generically, to different groupings, they share many features with the poetic form. Loy D. Martin has even suggested that the 'drunkalogue' of an Alcoholics Anonymous meeting, where a member stands up to tell the story of his or her problems with alcohol and, where appropriate, the story of his or her recovery, is a device formally very like the poetic dramatic monologue. The story, he observes, is always the same, with only minor rearrangement of episodes, and the purpose of these 'drunkalogues' is 'to destroy the illusion of the uniqueness of the self and to impress each member with the fact that he or she has become no more than the embodiment of the most predictable of types' (Martin 1985: 260–1). The growing familiarity of the public with variations on monologue conventions may well have contributed to making the poetic form of the dramatic monologue particularly accessible. In turn, given the increasingly politicised nature of contemporary poetry, its status as social discourse, this accessibility may have prompted many poets to appropriate the form once more. In the introduction to the above-mentioned *The New Poetry*, an anthology of British poetry from the 1980s and early 1990s, the editors note how the poetry of this time 'reaffirms the arts' significance as public utterance' (Hulse *et al.* 1993: 16). Social and cultural critique, many now believe, requires a democratically accessible form, and the dramatic monologue would therefore appear a far more useful tool for social critique than such experimental forms as, say, language-centred poetry, which risks being understood by only a limited 'elite'.

Social critique would appear to be the point of the majority of dramatic monologues written over the past twenty years, including such frequently anthologised poems as Duncan Bush's 'Pneumoconiosis' (1985), in which a miner speaks of his destroyed lungs; his later 'Are There Still Wolves in Pennsylvania' (1994), a sequence of monologues spoken by a disturbed American Vietnam War veteran and his wife; and Paula Meehan's 'The Statue of the Virgin at Granard Speaks' (1991), prompted by the fifteen-year-old Irish girl who died alone, giving birth, along with her baby. These monologues exploit the form's dynamic of self and context to draw attention to specific social problems, pointedly criticising the state and the way the state deals with the individual.

This is not to say that the lyric, another conventional form with which many readers are now familiar, has been completely jettisoned in the growing emphasis on poetry as socially responsible public utterance. Many poets appear to have no hesitation in using the lyric 'I' to offer a personal response to issues of public concern. A significant number of others, however, prefer to speak through personae or characters, detaching poetic self from speaking 'I', or at least to problematise the question of voice, suggesting that the personal authoritative voice of the traditional lyric provides a somewhat inadequate response to the problems of the modern world.

In a move reminiscent of the Victorian reaction to the Romantic lyric voice, a number of contemporary poets have reacted against the kind of poetry of the self which has come to be associated with such older poets as Ted Hughes. Ian McMillan's 'Ted Hughes is Elvis Presley' (1991), for example, uses dramatic monologue to question the cult of personality and the role of poetry in today's world, and to challenge the type of poetry which is, to adapt the phrase of McMillan's Elvis/Ted, all about 'great bulbous me' (55). Written at a time when Hughes was Poet Laureate, the monologue merges poet superstar with rock-and-roll superstar as the speaker, Elvis, confirms that indeed he did not die. Rather, he faked it, headed for London, found 'a guy, big guy, guy with a briefcase' (39), and knifed him:

> as the blood shot
> I became him
> like momma used to say
> the loaf became Jesus.
> (42–5)

What Hughes produces, McMillan suggests through this monologue, is ultimately, like Elvis, the music of the self (55), a point made particularly clear by the echoes of Hughes's 'Pike' (1959) in the final lines:

> I sit here,
> I can feel the evening shrinking me
> smaller and smaller.
> I have almost gone. Ted,
> three inches long, perfect.
> Elvis, Ted.
>
> (74–9)

At the same time as McMillan criticises the poetry of the self associated with Hughes in this monologue, he also makes explicit the strategies of his own poetic form: Elvis becomes 'Ted' as writing poet becomes speaking character.

One of the most distinctive features of the contemporary dramatic monologue is indeed the way it tends to expose and make explicit so many of the conventions of the form. Carol Ann Duffy's 'The Dummy' (1987), for example, which gives the ventriloquist's dummy a voice of its own, is precisely concerned with the split between speaking subject and the subject position which is assumed in the articulation of voice. Many contemporary monologues play with the distinction between poetic and speaking voice. In Jo Shapcott's 'Phrase Book' (1992) the opening line suggests unmediated lyric: 'I'm standing here inside my skin' (1). The speaker appears to be the poet, in her 'own front room' (4), watching live coverage of a war on television. At the same time, however, the speaking 'I' soon appears to be a fictionalised English tourist. Shapcott's problematisation of voice works to emphasise the instability and confusion of a post-imperial England no longer able to control the world and uncertain of its own place and position:

> Where is the British Consulate? Please explain.
> What does it mean? What must I do? Where
> can I find? What have I done? I have done
> nothing. Let me pass please. I am an Englishwoman.
>
> (33–6)

The fluidity of the speaking voice is emphasised by the monologue's more general refusal to remain limited to any one meaning. Lines from a travel phrasebook are offered throughout, and are repeatedly opposed to their possible alternatives: 'You are right. You are wrong. / Things are going well (badly). Am I disturbing you?' (7–8). Well, yes, and that seems to be the point: we are offered no fixed position from which to interpret this speaker; we are discouraged from identifying with any unified subject.

The problematising of the speaking 'I' caused by the reader's constant awareness of the pressure of the poet's controlling mind is, of course, already evident in Victorian dramatic monologues, and intensified in the modernist monologue. It is, however, something that becomes an increasingly self-conscious strategy in contemporary variations of the form and usually works to foreground the processes of representation. Poets use the dramatic monologue to expose the conflicting and multiple positions through which the self can be situated and to emphasise the ways in which this self is produced by various socioeconomic and linguistic systems. In Carol Ann Duffy's 'Translating the English 1989' (1990), for example, there is absolutely no attempt to create even the illusion of 'character': the speaker is clearly nothing more than the product of various conflicting discourses. 'Welcome to my country!' (1), the speaker begins, and then proceeds to list a confusing catalogue of what is on offer. 'Daffodils (Wordsworth. Up North)' (4), Shakespeare and the Opera are mixed in with wheel clamps, the black market and the football hooligan. 'Also we can be talking crack, smack / and Carling Black Label if we are so inclined' (11–12). Precisely because the various items are so incongruously brought together, and placed on an equal level, Duffy draws our attention to the way in which an acceptable version of English identity is more usually constructed through selectively eliminating some of the undesirable representations.

REVISIONIST DRAMATIC MONOLOGUES

The emphasis on questions of representation is particularly notable in contemporary revisionist monologues, monologues which draw upon characters from literature, history or myth in order to demonstrate how cultural beliefs and traditions have been fixed and formalised. Glyn Maxwell's *Out of the Rain* (1992), for example, contains 'The Thief on the Cross' and a series of monologues entitled 'The Beast and Beauty', in which the Beast himself speaks. It is, however, women poets who most frequently use the monologue to engage in revisionary myth-making, and their monologues are often highly polemical. Since the late 1970s, many women have exploited the form of the monologue to give voices to those who were silenced or to subvert patriarchal representations of women. In Rita Ann Higgins's 'Donna Laura' (1996), for example, Petrarch the great lover and writer of sonnets appears nothing but a swaggering poser; in 'Galileo's Wife' (1993) Lavinia Greenlaw engages with questions of gender and different ways of formulating knowledge as she lets the wife of the man usually hailed as the Father of Modern Science tell her side of the story. Such poems place themselves within a tradition that can be seen to originate with such monologues as Augusta Webster's 'Circe' or Amy Levy's 'Xantippe'. What makes many contemporary revisionary monologues different, however, is their increasing emphasis on the poet's controlling mind and their consequent exposure of issues of representation. While the earlier poets only indirectly call forth the contemporary context, only obliquely comment upon middle-class Victorian women's existence, later poets often overtly provide an incongruous mixture of their speaker's world and their own world.

While Amy Levy attempts to create the illusion of a woman's world in ancient Greece through both language and context, for example, there is quite a different effect when Rita Ann Higgins's speaker addresses Plato in 'The Flute Girl' (1996). Not only does she complain about the way he treats her and other women, she also makes him aware she knows precisely what he and his friends are up to, sitting four on a couch that 'seats two comfortably' and 'acting the maggot' (12). ' "Discourse in Praise of Love" indeed' (5), she sneers:

> Let me tell you Big Sandals
> the Flute Girl's had it
> When I get the sisters in here
> we are going to sit on the lot of you
> come out then gushing platonic
>
> (22–6)

as such modern idioms as 'acting the maggot' (Irish slang for shirking work) and 'the sisters' invade the flute girl's monologue, the voice seems to move between poet and speaker, further complicating the already complex strategy of the feint. The signals gesturing towards the poet are as clear as those gesturing towards the speaker. Language creates a similarly jarring effect in the four monologues of U.A. Fanthorpe's 'Only Here for the Bier' (1982), which attempt to show, as she explains, 'how the masculine world of Shakespeare's tragedies would look from the woman's angle' (49). Contemporary revisionist writers of monologues, like many Victorian poets, may appropriate the voice of a known figure from a historical, mythical or literary world, but instead of providing a language recognisably specific to the speaker they use a language associated with the poet's own world. The pressure of the poet's controlling mind, frequently felt in the Victorian monologue through the poem's form, is now intensified through the poem's language. This emphasises the act of representation, exposing the speaker as nothing more than a construct. And this in turn draws attention to the culture which has produced that speaker, the world of the poet, allowing for social critique.

The technique is further developed in Carol Ann Duffy's more recent collection of monologues, *The World's Wife* (1999). 'Mrs Aesop', for example, offers a strikingly new and eminently convincing perspective on Aesop and his fables. 'By Christ, he could bore for Purgatory' 1), she begins, and 'let me tell you now / that the bird in his hand shat on his sleeve, / never mind the two worth less in the bush. Tedious' 3–4). These opening lines reproduce many of the strategies considered typical of Browning's monologues, most notably the abrupt beginning, which places us right in the middle of a situation, and the colloquial language. But colloquial though it may be, Mrs Aesop's chatty voice does not sound like the voice of the wife of a Phrygian slave, and certainly not like the voice of a woman who lived around 600 BC. Past and present become conflated by Duffy's monologue; this is a Mrs Aesop who has been transported to the late twentieth century. The worlds of the speaker and the poet become fused, while, paradoxically, the split between poet and speaker is simultaneously further emphasised. As in the case of Higgins, there is no attempt to create the illusion of a 'real' speaking person here; we can never forget that what we are offered is the poet's representation of that speaking subject.

Furthermore, Duffy conflates the old fables with new ones as sh introduces the anachronisms which signal towards the poet's own con text. In the final lines of 'Mrs Aesop', when the frustrated wife i explaining how dreadful the sex was with her husband, she tells u about the fable that she made up 'about a little cock that wouldn't crow (22). '*I'll cut off your tale, all right,* I said, *to save my face*', she concludes 'That shut him up. I laughed last, longest' (24–5).

There would seem to be a not so subtle reference here to Lorett Bobbett, notorious for cutting off her husband's penis, and most reader would have found it difficult to remain oblivious of this event, give that it was so highly publicised in the media. It is such references tha point to one of the most innovative developments in the form of th dramatic monologue today, and that demonstrate most clearly the way in which this particular genre has developed and changed in response t specific historical and cultural conditions. Contemporary monologue repeatedly and directly draw upon and respond to media events.

DRAMATIC MONOLOGUES AND THE MEDIA

In *New Relations: The Refashioning of British Poetry 1980–1994*, Davi Kennedy introduces the idea of what he calls 'poetry as media', a term which suggests a 'wider range of activity, commentary and responsive ness than a designation such as "political poetry" would cove (Kennedy 1996: 214). Although by no means a new phenomenon, h suggests, there was a notable increase in such writing during the 1980 and 1990s. This increase he sees as the product of a set of specific cul tural conditions in late twentieth-century Western culture, including most significantly for my discussion here, the rise of global electroni media.

The rise of these media, I would add, has had a significant effec upon the writing of the dramatic monologue. If the conventions of th monologue appear to have spilled over into the media, the media hav had an equivalent influence upon the monologue. Late twentieth-cen tury equivalents of Browning's 'Porphyria's Lover' are quite likely to giv voice to actual psychopaths, confident that the reader will recognise th speaker. Ken Smith's 'Brady at Saddleworth Moor' (1990), for example is the first in a trilogy of three poems about British murderers, 'Figure in Three Landscapes'. The monologue alludes to the time when the Moors murderer was taken by the police to the scene of his crimes in the hope he might aid in the solving of other murders, and it would appear to be precisely because this poem is written in the form of the monologue that it has received so much attention, and appears so troubling. Murderers like Brady and his accomplice Myra Hindley, as David Kennedy observes, 'are staples of the tabloid press', and Smith plays down the usual sensationalism by making only indirect references to the crimes and instead presenting the poem as the words of Brady himself (Kennedy 1996: 222). And yet the speaker becomes all the more disturbing as the use of the monologue suggests his 'humanity', implies he has emotions and desires and feelings. The self-consciously poetic nature of the language contributes further to the humanising of the mass murderer as Brady revels in the air, the wind, the sky and the wide open spaces experienced during his hours of freedom.

Many poets use speakers familiar to the reader through the media, though these are not always as chilling as Brady. Jo Shapcott in *Phrase Book* (1992), for example, draws upon speakers as diverse as Superman, Marlon Brando, the cartoon cat from Tom and Jerry, and a whole series of mad cows. It is a strategy, however, that can be particularly associated with the dramatic monologues of the American poet Ai. Ai has habitually used the dramatic monologue since her first collection of poetry, *Cruelty*, was published in 1973, and almost from the start she has drawn upon well-known figures for her speakers. She usually chooses those who have been somehow particularly fixed and trapped by cultural definition, and her monologues work to disturb these definitions. These speakers generally fall into one or more of three categories. The first group can be roughly described as in some way iconic figures, including Marilyn Monroe, Elvis Presley, Lenny Bruce and James Dean. The second group consists of speakers from the world of politics, including Richard Nixon, Jimmy Hoffa, Jack Ruby and Bill Clinton. The third group contains socially marginalised figures, including both victimisers like the rapist, the murderer, the paedophile, and their victims, such as the abused wife or child. While a few of the speakers in this third group appear relatively generalised types, others are specified, or, as with 'The Good Shepherd, Atlanta, 1981' (1986), and 'Charisma' (1999), with its reference to Waco, Texas, enough details are provided to link the speakers with cases that have been well publicised in the media: a certain amount of knowledge on the reader's part is assumed.

With a number of Ai's monologues, the reader is forced into playing a more than usually active role. This produces an often disturbing sense of complicity since if Browning approaches what his Bishop Blougram called 'the dangerous edge of things', Ai has a decided tendency to spring over that edge. 'False Witness' (1999), for example, shows why Ai may well feel the need to subtitle many of her monologues as 'A Fiction', and why the copyright page of her publications insists that her dramatic monologues are '100 percent fiction', even if '[s]ome of them project the names of "real" public figures onto made-up characters in made-up circumstances.'

'False Witness' is spoken by a mother to her young daughter, a daughter whom she encourages her husband to abuse sexually. This is something which we are invited to witness rather too closely for comfort as the last section moves into the present tense to relate one particular moment of abuse. Although the speaker is never identified by name, from its very opening this monologue is suggestive of a high-profile murder :

> I did not buy you the tiara
> with the fake jewels,
> because your father said it made you look cheap,
> although eventually, he confessed
> that he was thrilled to think of you wearing only tap shoes
> and your crown of silver plate and paste.
>
> (1–6)

Tiaras and tap shoes will make it difficult for many readers not to think immediately of six-year-old JonBenét Ramsey, the Little Miss Colorado who was discovered murdered in the basement of her parents' home on Christmas night in 1996. The case was never solved. A grand jury met for over a year only to disband in 1999 without handing down an indictment or even issuing a report. Although suspicion was immediately cast upon the Ramseys, they were never tried; many, however, have openly accused the mother, including Steve Thomas, a Boulder city detective who worked on the case.

As Ai insists, however, this poem is clearly 'A Fiction'. Not only are the speaker and her daughter and husband nameless, but even if the reader connects the situation with the Ramsey case, this remains a fictional reconstruction; no one knows either what led to the murder of JonBenét or the identity of the murderer. Nevertheless, a number of details throughout the monologue echo details from the case which were well publicised. JonBenét was garrotted with a cord, for example, and here the mother ominously puts a rope around her daughter's neck; JonBenét was discovered with vaginal trauma, and here the mother takes a stick, inserts it and twists. Such details, however, are interwoven with literary sources, including Dickens's *Great Expectations*, to move the poem beyond the one specific event and consider some of the more general issues underlying child abuse. The mother who speaks colludes with, even initiates, her husband's sexual exploitation of the child; she has brought up the child precisely for this purpose, tutoring her 'in the art of seduction' (45). When her husband observes 'he didn't know a six year old / could be such a cruel mistress' (30–1), she tells him, echoing Miss Havisham's comment on Estella, 'Making men suffer is her destiny' (32). The desire for power, over others and over herself, repeatedly emerges as central to the speaker's actions, but no easy solutions are offered as to why the woman acts in this way. She may have been abused herself as a child, but this is something of which she is uncertain: 'sometimes I think that nothing happened / when my father said good night' (50–1), and she recognises she may well be 'an unreliable witness to my own life' (54). She can no longer even identify her past self when she sifts through her guilt trying 'to find the woman / who became a mother / with no other thought than of revenge' (41–3). There is no true self that can be accessed here; personal memory is either unreliable or has been corrupted.

Even when Ai uses speakers who are not so clearly suggestive of actual public figures, the media continue to play a central role since her monologues appropriate not only public figures and events but also various types of media discourse. A similar point can be made about the monologues of Carol Ann Duffy, who, like Ai, has regularly used this particular generic form. From one perspective it might be argued that the monologues of Ai and Duffy are very different: Duffy is frequently celebrated for her adeptness in manipulating the colloquial voice and for her variety of styles; Ai, on the other hand, is often accused of not distinguishing her speakers through voice and instead having them all speak in the same flat monotone. This assessment of Ai's voices is perhaps not, however, quite fair or accurate; even if Ai does not use such blatantly colloquial language as Duffy, both poets in fact repeatedly explore the ways in which our socio-cultural contexts, and particularly our language, can be said to produce us as subjects.

In this respect, the similarities in both the strategies and the concerns of the two poets can be best seen by considering two monologues in which they use psychopathic speakers: Ai's 'The Kid' (1979) and Duffy's 'Psychopath' (1987). Duffy's speaker keeps returning to the past, focusing on what might have caused the young man's psychotic behaviour, including his early sexual experiences. We get little detail about any actual act of murder; rather, descriptions of moments leading up to a murder are juxtaposed with the repeated phrase 'She is in the canal'. It is the romanticised media constructs of outlaw masculinity, however, which seem primarily responsible for the production of this speaking subject, as the psychopath repeatedly identifies with such figures as James Dean, Elvis, Little Richard and Marlon Brando, and uses lines associated with such figures as Humphrey Bogart: 'Here's / looking at you' (57–8) he tells his reflection. Repeatedly, his language suggests both the innocently naïve and the corrupt. When he claims it is 'Easier to stay a child, wide-eyed; / at the top of the helter-skelter' (51–2), for example, it is not just the fair-ground spiral slide which comes to mind, but also the mass murderer Charles Manson, who used the term 'helter-skelter' to refer to what he considered to be a coming race war and left the words scrawled on the refrigerator after the murder of Sharon Tate.

Ai's monologue retains the present tense throughout, showing rather than telling us the circumstances which have contributed to the boy's violent outburst, involving us directly in the murders that follow, and forcing us to witness the actual brutality of the psychopath. This is something Ai does throughout her many dramatic monologues, repeatedly drawing our attention to, and forcing us to witness, the horrific violence that she presents as such an integral part of American culture. The very title of 'The Kid' draws attention to her specific focus here: the romanticisation of violence by the media, and particularly of the

igure of the outlaw. Like Duffy, she is interested in the way that popu-
ar media myths might covertly make such violence legitimate.

The opening stanza suggests a cause for, at the same time as it antici-
ates, the eruption of violence to follow. As the speaker's sister sits in
he truck, he walks around 'hitting the flat tires with an iron rod' (4).
The father shouts at him, the mother calls, he picks up a rock and
hrows it at the kitchen window, and 'The old man's voice bounces off
he air like a ball / I can't lift my leg over' (10–11). These brief opening
ines are indeed delivered in the flat tone of which so many reviewers
ave complained, but they function well in conveying a striking sense
f boredom, frustration and entrapment. Abruptly in the second stanza
he violence explodes as the speaker splits open his father's skull with
he iron rod and then kills his mother with a blow to the spine.

With the release of violence there appears to come an accompanying
elease from the constricting identity formed by his environment; there
s now a sense of distance from his family; his sister becomes 'the one
ut back' (19) he has forgotten and goes back to shoot. His old identity
eems to dissolve and to be replaced by something free, unconstrained.
But as the clichés and fragments of nursery rhymes and popular songs
eem to suggest, this new identity is as much the product of the world
n which the speaker lives as the old one, and the shift in register in the
inal lines of the monologue emphasises the delusive nature of the freedom he thinks he has gained: 'Then I go outside and cross the fields to
he highway. / I'm fourteen. I'm a wind from nowhere. / I can break
our heart' (29–31).

This last line draws attention to an interesting manipulation of the
peaker/auditor convention. As in so many contemporary examples of
he form, there appears to be no actual auditor in this monologue, so to
whose heart does he refer? Much the same point can be made about
Psychopath'. Although Duffy's speaker frequently addresses his own
eflection, he also seems to be talking to someone else. 'Let me make
myself crystal' (5), he says, but to whom is he concerned to make himself
lear? Both poems remain marked by the signs of communication, and
would appear to be addressed to someone else, but there is no auditor
resent. While it is certainly true that many Victorian and Modernist
monologues do not have auditors, this lack of an auditor combined with
 direct address to an unspecified 'you' seems a particularly late

twentieth-century development. 'The Kid' and 'Psychopath' are typical of many contemporary monologues in the way they eliminate the audience in the poem and have the speaking 'I' directly address the reader, pulling the reader further in to the speaker's world and, by implication, into a confrontation with the problems of modern society. It may be that this is partly related to the way in which developments in media technology generally have gradually affected the dynamics of the speaker/auditor relationship in our society. With radio and television, an audience can be addressed without being present, something which has been intensified with the advent of the internet, where, in various 'chat rooms', totally fictional personae can be constructed and presented.

With the monologues of such contemporary poets as Duffy and Ai we have come a long way from Browning's duke telling the envoy about his last duchess, and a long way from anything that could be usefully be considered in terms of such issues as revelation of character or dramatic irony. The way in which the monologue has developed seems to confirm what both Herbert Tucker and Isobel Armstrong have suggested in their investigations into the origins of the genre: that what is primarily important about the form is the way it engages with the dynamic of self and context. In appropriating this dynamic for the purposes of social critique, and in emphasising the issues of representation and communication, contemporary poets ensure that the monologue remains a relevant and useful form. The apparent decline of the genre in the hands of such Modernist poets as Eliot and Pound consequently comes to seem no more than a minor blip in the development of a still vital genre.

But what of such issues as revelation of character and dramatic irony? Have developments in theory rendered them, from the perspective of both poet and critic, completely irrelevant to all contemporary monologues? Perhaps not quite all, but to see these in action it may be necessary to turn to the spin-dominated world of politics. 'It is a little known fact', Peter Forbes wrote, that

> the techniques of the persuaders – government spin doctors, media advisers, advertisers – are very closely allied to poetry. At a time when poetry is sidelined in our culture, a perversion of its techniques has become a powerful tool in shaping our perceptions.
>
> (Forbes 1993: 2)

While I suspect the general proposition here may be debatable, Forbes's comment invites us to consider how applicable this might be to the dramatic monologue in particular, a form that is in itself so frequently concerned with persuasion of one kind or another. Listening to some of the great political oratory of the twentieth century, such as Churchill's wartime speeches or Edward VII's abdication speech, the connections with dramatic monologue seem quite striking. This is, no doubt, partly because the persuasive dramatic monologue is, in some ways, always rhetoric, but also partly because many political speakers assume specific personae for the purposes of specific occasions. To take a more recent example, can there ever have been a more public performance of a dramatic monologue than when Bill Clinton went on television to persuade the world of his innocence in the Monica Lewinsky affair? All the old characteristics that used to define the form appear: we have a speaker, a whole series of auditors unable to query or respond, and even, in retrospect, unintentional revelation of character and decided dramatic irony. It may well be significant that one of the very few monologues in which Ai does strikingly exploit dramatic irony is her recent 'Blood in the Water' (1999), subtitled 'A Fiction', with the epigraph 'written after learning about a presidential affair'. In terms of monomania, the unrepentant speaker here rivals Browning's duke: 'I am the captain of this ship of state,' he concludes with a clear and appropriate echo of W.E. Henley's 'Invictus' (1875), 'and I will sail us through the stormy seas of sleaze, / or we will all go down together / on our knees' (86–9). Browning would have loved it.

GLOSSARY

Aestheticism A movement in the arts, including literature, during the second half of the nineteenth century. Proponents of Aestheticism considered that art had no function beyond itself: they believed it was politically, socially and personally disengaged and should be judged purely by aesthetic criteria.

Anaphora A rhetorical device in which a word or phrase is repeated in successive clauses, usually at the beginning of sentences in prose or at the start of lines in poetry. This is an example from Tennyson's 'The Lady of Shalott' (1842): 'She left the web, she left the loom, / She made three paces thro' the room, / She saw the water-lily bloom' (109–11).

Caesura A pause within a line of verse. In the following example from Arnold's 'Dover Beach' (1867), there is a caesura in the middle of the first line and this line is enjambed, or run on, into the second line, which has an even heavier caesura in the middle: 'The tide is full, the moon lies fair / Upon the straits; – on the French coast the light / Gleams and is gone ...' (2–4).

Concrete poetry Poetry in which typography is used to display the subject of a poem through its form.

Decadence A term generally applied to any culture in decline, but more specifically associated with literature *c*. 1870–1900, particularly in France, that cultivated the artificial and rejected the natural, and frequently focused upon the strange or the perverse.

Deconstruction A concept primarily associated with the French philosopher Jacques Derrida. It is a strategy whereby systems of thought and concepts are dismantled in such a way as to expose the contradictions and divisions at the heart of meaning.

Dialogic Term derived from the work of Russian theorist Mikhail Bakhtin. Generally speaking, it refers to the polyphonic play of different voices or discourses within a text.

Dramatic irony Often a feature of plays, dramatic irony occurs when the audience has more information about what is occurring than do the characters themselves. In the dramatic monologue it is the result of the disjunction between the limited understanding of the speaker and the wider awareness of the poet and the reader.

End-stopped line A line of verse in which the end of the line coincides with an essential grammatical pause (as opposed to an enjambed line). The following three lines from Tennyson's 'St Simeon Stylites' (1842) are all end-stopped: 'O Lord, thou knowest what a man I am; / A sinful man, conceived and born in sin: / 'Tis their own doing: this is none of mine;' (118–20).

Enjambement A line of poetry in which the sentence continues into the next line without any grammatical pause. The first three lines in the following example from Tennyson's 'Ulysses' (1842) are enjambed, and the fourth line is end-stopped: 'Push off, and, sitting well in order, smite / The sounding furrows; for my purpose holds / To sail beyond the sunset, and the baths / Of all the western stars, until I die.' (58–61).

Epistemology The branch of philosophy which is concerned with the grounds and forms of knowledge.

Feint A term coined by narratologist Käte Hamburger in 1957 to describe the effect of a first-person fictional narrative. Since the 'I' who writes uses the conventions of ordinary language, addresses someone, and does not exploit those signals by which we normally identify fiction, such as access to the thoughts of others, the first-person narrative is a feigned reality statement. The term was appropriated by Alan Sinfield in 1977 to describe the effect of the speaker in the dramatic monologue.

Formalism Formalist criticism ignores the feelings of the writer, the response of the reader and the relationship of the text to its context, and focuses instead on artistic structure and form. The Russian formalist movement started around 1917 and considered the ways in which elements in a specific text creatively deviate from those established by literary norms and conventions (see also New Critics).

Hegemony A term primarily associated with the Italian Marxist Antonio Gramsci and which, generally speaking, refers to the ways in which a dominant group negotiates its position with those other groups in society over whom it seeks to exert power.

Ideology   Systems of cultural assumptions or the set of opinions, values and beliefs of a group of people which uphold or oppose social order and power and which may disguise the contradictory elements in a social formation.

Metonymy   A figure of speech in which an attribute of a thing, or something associated with it, is substituted for the thing itself. An example would be the phrase 'the pen is mightier than the sword', where the pen is literature and the sword war.

Modernism   The label given to a movement in early twentieth-century art and literature which broke with the 'realist' tradition of the nineteenth century and is particularly marked by experimentalism in form.

New Critics   A formalist movement of the 1930s and 1940s in America which asserted the autonomy of literature, practised close reading of texts and saw all the elements of a particular text ideally converging within a unified whole.

Pathetic fallacy   A term first used by John Ruskin in 1856 to describe the habit, common among poets, of assuming an equation between their own mood and the surrounding world.

Phenomenology   School of thought founded by German philosopher Edmund Husserl which maintains that objects attain meaning through their perception in an individual's consciousness.

Romantic   The Romantic period is generally considered to begin around 1789, with the French Revolution, and to end around 1830.

Subject/subjectivity   The notion of the 'subject' is part of a movement away from the humanist conception of the autonomous and stable individual. The self as a subject is situated in and by language and by various cultural and social discourses and institutions. Also contained within the concept of the 'subject' is the notion of subjection, which introduces questions about the ways in which individual behaviour is conditioned by external forces.

Synaesthesia The description of a sense impression in terms more appropriate to a different sense, or the mixing of sense impressions. One of the most notable examples is John Keats's description of wine in 'Ode to a Nightingale' (1820): 'Tasting of Flora and the country green, / Dance, and Provençal song, and sunburnt mirth!' (13–14).

Victorian The period spanning the reign of Queen Victoria, lasting from 1837 until 1901, but frequently taken back to include the 1830s, during which many of the most notable Victorian writers, including Browning and Tennyson, began to write.

BIBLIOGRAPHY

Poems are documented by line number. When no modern edition of a poet's work is available, whenever possible poems are sourced from modern anthologies and the following abbreviations are used:

VWP: Leighton, A. and Reynolds M. (eds) (1995) *Victorian Women Poets: An Anthology*, Oxford: Blackwell.
VWP2: Blain, V. (ed.) (2001) *Victorian Women Poets*, Harlow: Pearson.

For all other works cited, the Harvard referencing system has been used and details are given below.

Primary sources

Ai (1999) *Vice: New and Selected Poems*, New York: Norton.
Arnold, M. (1979) *Arnold: The Complete Poems*, ed. M. Allott, Harlow: Longman.
Barrett Browning, E. (1900) *The Complete Works of Elizabeth Barrett Browning*, eds C. Porter and H.A. Clarke, New York: Thomas Crowell.
Bennett, A. (1988) *Talking Heads*, London: BBC Books.
Brooks, G. (1987) *Blacks*, Chicago: David.
Browning, R. (1970) *Poetical Works 1833–1864*, ed. I. Jack, Oxford: Oxford University Press.
—— (1981) *The Ring and the Book*, ed. R.D. Altick, Harmondsworth: Penguin.
Bush, D. (1985) *Salt*, Bridgend: Seren Books
—— (1994) *Masks*, Bridgend: Poetry Wales Press.
Duffy, C.A. (1987) *Selling Manhattan*, London: Anvil.
—— (1990) *The Other Country*, London: Anvil.
—— (1999) *The World's Wife*, London: Picador.
Eliot, T.S. (1971) *The Complete Poems and Plays, 1909–1950*, New York: Harcourt Brace.
Fanthorpe, U.A. (1982) *Standing To*, Liskeard: Peterloo Poets.
Greenlaw, L. (1993) *Night Photograph*, London: Faber.
Hemans, F. (1849) *Poems of Felicia Hemans*, Edinburgh: Blackwood.
Higgins, R.A. (1996) *Sunny Side Plucked. New and Selected Poems*, Newcastle upon Tyne: Bloodaxe.
Howard, R. (1969) *Untitled Subjects*, New York: Athenaeum.
Hughes, L. (1949) *One-Way Ticket*, New York: Alfred A. Knopf.
King, Roma A., Jr (ed.) (1981) *The Complete Works of Robert Browning*, Vol. 5, Athens, OH: Ohio University Press.

Kingsley, C. (1897) *Poems*, London: Macmillan.

Kipling, R. (1966) *Collected Verse*, London: Hodder and Stoughton.

Landon, L.E. (1997) *Letitia Elizabeth Landon. Selected Writings*, eds J. McGann and D. Riess, Peterborough: Broadview Press.

Levy, A. (1993) *The Complete Novels and Selected Writings of Amy Levy 1861–1889*, ed. M. New, Gainesville, FL: University Press of Florida.

Lowell, R. (1946) *Lord Weary's Castle*, New York: Harcourt Brace.

—— (1951) *The Mills of the Kavanaughs*, New York: Harcourt Brace.

—— (1959) *Life Studies*, New York: Farrar, Straus and Giroux, 1970.

McMillan, I. (1991) *A Chin*, Huddersfield: Wide Skirt Press.

Masters, E.L. (1916) *Spoon River Anthology*, New York: Macmillan.

Maxwell, G. (1992) *Out of the Rain*, Newcastle upon Tyne: Bloodaxe.

Meehan, P. (1991) *The Man who was Marked by Winter*, Oldcastle: Gallery Press.

Mew, C. (1982) *Collected Poems and Prose*, ed. V. Warner, London: Virago.

Morgan, E. (1990) *Collected Poems*, Manchester: Carcanet.

Morris, W. (1904) *The Defence of Guenevere and Other Poems*, ed. R. Steele, London: De La More Press.

Parker, A.M. and Willhardt, M. (eds) (1996) *The Routledge Anthology of Cross-Gendered Verse*, London: Routledge.

Phillips, S. (1918) 'Penelope to Ulysses', in T.H. Ward (ed.) *The English Poets*, Vol. 5, London: Macmillan, 552–3.

Pound, E. (1926) *Personae. The Collected Shorter Poems of Ezra Pound*, New York: New Directions.

Rossetti, D.G. (1891) *The Complete Poetical Works of Dante Gabriel Rossetti*, ed. W.M. Rossetti, London: Elvey.

Shapcott, J. (1992) *Phrase Book*, Oxford: Oxford University Press.

Smith, K. (1990) *The Heart, The Border*, Newcastle upon Tyne: Bloodaxe.

Swinburne, A.C. (1900) *Poems and Ballads*, London: Chatto and Windus.

Tennyson, A. (1969) *The Poems of Tennyson*, ed. C. Ricks, London: Longman.

Webster, A. (2000) *Augusta Webster: Portraits and Other Poems*, ed. C. Sutphin, Peterborough, Ont.: Broadview Press.

Secondary sources

Abrams, M.H. (1958) *The Mirror and the Lamp: Romantic Theory and the Critical Tradition*, New York: Norton.

—— (1965) 'Structure and Style in the Greater Romantic Lyric', in F.W. Hilles and H. Bloom (eds) *From Sensibility to Romanticism*, Oxford: Oxford University Press, 527–60.

—— (1973) *Natural Supernaturalism. Tradition and Revolution in Romantic Literature*, New York: Norton.

Anderson, A. (1989) 'D.G. Rossetti's "Jenny": Agency, Intersubjectivity, and the Prostitute', *Genders* 4: 103–21.

Armstrong, I. (1993) *Victorian Poetry. Poetry, Poetics and Politics*, London: Routledge.

Bloom, H. (ed.) (1985) *Robert Browning. Modern Critical Views*, New York: Chelsea House.

Bristow, J. (ed.) (1987) *The Victorian Poet: Poetics and Persona*, London: Croom Helm.

—— (2000) *The Cambridge Companion to Victorian Poetry*, Cambridge: Cambridge University Press.

Butler, J. (1990) *Gender Trouble. Feminism and the Subversion of Identity*, London: Routledge.

Christ, C. (1984) *Victorian and Modern Poetics*, Chicago: University of Chicago Press.

Cohen, R. (1986) 'History and Genre', *New Literary History*, 17, 2: 203–18.

Cunningham, V. (ed.) (2000) *The Victorians. An Anthology of Poetry and Poetics*, Oxford: Blackwell.

Derrida, J. (1992) 'The Law of Genre', in D. Attridge (ed.) *Acts of Literature*, London: Routledge, 221–52.

Duff, D. (ed.) (2000) *Modern Genre Theory*, London: Longman.

Faas, E. (1988) *Retreat Into the Mind. Victorian Poetry and the Rise of Psychiatry*, Princeton: Princeton University Press.

Flint, K. (1996) ' "...As A Rule, I Does Not Mean I". Personal Identity and the Victorian Woman Poet', in R. Porter (ed.) *ReWriting the Self. Histories from the Renaissance to the Present*, London: Routledge, 156–66.

Forbes, P. (1993) 'New Ageism', *The Guardian*, 26 May, Arts section: 4–5

Fuson, B.W. (1948) *Browning and His English Predecessors in the Dramatic Monolog*, Iowa City: State University of Iowa Humanistic Studies, Vol. 8.

Gregson, I. (1996) *Contemporary Poetry and Postmodernism*, Basingstoke: Macmillan.

Howe, E.A. (1996) *The Dramatic Monologue*, New York: Twayne.

Hughes, L.K. (ed.) (1984) *The Dramatic 'I' Poem*. Special Issue of *Victorian Poetry*, 22, 2.

—— (1987) *The Manyfacèd Glass. Tennyson's Dramatic Monologues*, Athens: Ohio University Press.

Hulse, M., Kennedy, D. and Morley, D. (1993) 'Introduction', in M. Hulse, D. Kennedy and D. Morley, *The New Poetry*, Newcastle upon Tyne: Bloodaxe, 15–28.

Hyder, C.K. (ed.) (1966) *Swinburne Replies*, Syracuse, NY: Syracuse University Press.

—— (1970) *Swinburne: The Critical Heritage*, New York: Barnes and Noble.

Kennedy, D. (1996) *New Relations: The Refashioning of British Poetry 1980–1994*, Bridgend: Poetry Wales Press.

Knoepflmacher, U.C. (1984) 'Projection and the Female Other: Romanticism, Browning, and the Victorian Dramatic Monologue', *Victorian Poetry*, 22, 2: 139–59.

Langbaum, R. (1957) *The Poetry of Experience. The Dramatic Monologue in Modern Literary Tradition*, London: Chatto and Windus.

Leighton, A. (1992) *Victorian Women Poets: Writing Against the Heart*, Hemel Hempstead: Harvester Wheatsheaf.

McGann, J. (1972) *Swinburne: An Experiment in Criticism*, Chicago: University of Chicago Press.

Martin, L.D. (1985) *Browning's Dramatic Monologues and the Post-Romantic Subject*, Baltimore: Johns Hopkins University Press

Maynard, J. (1992) 'Reading the Reader in Robert Browning's Dramatic Monologues', in M.E. Gibson (ed.) *Critical Essays on Robert Browning*, New York: G.K. Hall, 69–78.

Mellor, A. (1993) *Romanticism and Gender*, London: Routledge.

Mermin, D. (1983) *The Audience in the Poem. Five Victorian Poets*, New Brunswick, NJ: Rutgers University Press.

—— (1986) 'The Damsel, the Knight, and the Victorian Woman Poet', *Critical Inquiry*, 13: 64–80.

—— (1995) ' "The fruitful feud of hers and his": Sameness, Difference, and Gender in Victorian Poetry', *Victorian Poetry*, 33, 1: 149–65.

Mill, J.S. (1942) *The Spirit of the Age*, Chicago: University of Chicago Press.

—— (1976) *Essays on Poetry*, ed. F.P. Sharpless, Columbia: Columbia University Press.

Miller, J. Hillis (1963) *The Disappearance of God: Five Nineteenth-Century Writers*, Cambridge, MA: Belknap Press of Harvard University Press.

Morgan, T. (1988) 'Mixed Metaphor, Mixed Gender: Swinburne and the Victorian Critics', *Victorian Newsletter*, 73: 16–19.

Parry, A. (1988) 'Sexual Exploitation and Freedom: Religion, Race and Gender in Elizabeth Barrett Browning's "The Runaway Slave at Pilgrim's Point" ', *Studies in Browning and his Circle*, 16: 114–26.

Pearsall, C.D.J. (2000) 'The Dramatic Monologue', in J. Bristow (ed.) *The Cambridge Companion to Victorian Poetry*, Cambridge: Cambridge University Press, 67–88.

Pound, E. (1970) *Gaudier-Breska*, New York: New Directions.

Rader, R. (1976) 'The Dramatic Monologue and Related Lyric Forms', *Critical Inquiry*, 3: 131–51.

—— (1984) 'Notes on Some Structural Varieties and Variations in Dramatic "I" Poems and Their Theoretical Implications', *Victorian Poetry*, 22, 2: 103–20.

Rees-Jones, D. (1999) *Carol Ann Duffy*, Tavistock: Northcote House Publishers.

Riede, D.G. (1978) *Swinburne: A Study of Romantic Mythmaking*, Charlottesville: University of Virginia Press.

Riviere, J. (1986) 'Womanliness as a Masquerade', in V. Burgin, J. Donald and C. Kaplan (eds) *Formations of Fantasy*, London: Methuen, 25–44.

Scheinberg, C. (1997) 'Recasting "sympathy and judgment": Amy Levy, Women Poets, and the Victorian Dramatic Monologue', *Victorian Poetry*, 35, 2: 173–92.

Sessions, I.B. (1947) 'The Dramatic Monologue', *PMLA*, 62: 503–16.

Shaw, W.D. (1999) *Origins of the Monologue: The Hidden God*, Toronto: Toronto University Press.

Sieburth, R. (1984) 'Poetry and Obscenity: Baudelaire and Swinburne', *Comparative Literature*, 36, 4: 343–53.

Sinfield, A. (1977) *Dramatic Monologue*, London: Methuen.

Slinn, E.W. (1991) *The Discourse of Self in Victorian Poetry*, Charlottesville, VA: University Press of Virginia.

—— (1999) 'Poetry', in H.F. Tucker (ed.) *A Companion to Victorian Literature and Culture*, Oxford: Blackwell, 307–22.

Sussman, H. (1992) 'Robert Browning's "Fra Lippo Lippi" and the Problematic of a Male Poetic', *Victorian Studies*, 35, 2: 185–200.

Sutphin, C. (2000) 'Human Tigresses, Fractious Angels, and Nursery Saints: Augusta Webster's *A Castaway* and Victorian Discourses on Prostitution and Women's Sexuality', *Victorian Poetry*, 38, 4: 511–35.

Todorov, T. (1990) *Genres in Discourse*, trans. C. Porter, Cambridge: Cambridge University Press.

Tucker, H.F (1980) *Browning's Beginnings. The Art of Disclosure*, Minneapolis: University of Minnesota Press.

—— (1984) 'From Monomania to Monologue: "St Simeon Stylites" and the Rise of the Victorian Dramatic Monologue', *Victorian Poetry*, 22, 2: 121–37.

—— (1985) 'Dramatic Monologue and the Overhearing of Lyric', in C. Hosek and P. Parker (eds) *Lyric Poetry: Beyond New Criticism*, Ithaca, NY: Cornell University Press, 226–43.

—— (1988) *Tennyson and the Doom of Romanticism*, Cambridge, MA: Harvard University Press.

—— (1994) 'Wanted Dead or Alive: Browning's Historicism', *Victorian Poetry*, 38, 1: 25–40.

Watson, R. (1997) 'Edwin Morgan: Messages and Transformations', in G. Day and B. Docherty (eds) *British Poetry from the 1950s to the 1990s: Politics and Art*, Basingstoke: Macmillan, 170–92.

Wilde, O. (1989) *The Writings of Oscar Wilde*, ed. I. Murray, Oxford: Oxford University Press.

Wolfson, S.J. (1998) ' "Domestic Affections" and "the spear of Minerva": Felicia Hemans and the Dilemma of Gender', in C. Shiner Wilson and J. Haefner (eds) *Re-Visioning Romanticism: British Women Writers, 1776–1837*, Philadelphia: University of Pennsylvania Press, 128–66.

INDEX

CPSIA information can be obtained
at www.ICGtesting.com
Printed in the USA
FSOW02n2202260118
43845FS

9 780415 229371